SHOULD YOU TEACH
YOUR CHILDREN AT HOME?

Some readers may conclude that despite our disclaimers, we do in fact have an educational philosophy. If so, it is only that children *will* learn, *will* aspire to excellence, if we recognize and respect their different interests and abilities and give them a chance to develop them. In our view, every child is gifted one way or another. The tragedy is that this is denied every day, in word and in action, in our schools.

Homeschooling is not a panacea. But for increasing numbers of families it offers a degree of hope and opportunity. *Homeschooling for Excellence* is intended to provide a picture of one family's part in what has emerged as perhaps the most dynamic and creative educational movement in decades. We hope that our account will be of interest and helpful to parents of school-aged children and those who are charged with the task of educating them.

—David and Micki Colfax

HOMESCHOOLING FOR EXCELLENCE

David and Micki Colfax

WARNER BOOKS

A Time Warner Company

State laws, as they pertain to homeschooling, are subject to various interpretations by state and local school officials and the courts. Please refer to Appendix 5, "Homeschooling and the Law," for further information.

Warner Books Edition

This Warner Books edition is published by arrangement with Mountain House Press

Warner Books, Inc., 1271 Avenue of the Americas, New York, NY 10020

A Time Warner Company

Printed in the United States of America

First Warner Books Printing: October 1988

10

Book design by Nick Mazzella
Cover design by Harold Nolan
Cover photo: James Wilson/Woodfin Camp and Associates

Library of Congress Cataloging-in-Publication Data

Colfax, David.
 Homeschooling for excellence / David and Micki Colfax.—Warner Books ed.
  p. cm.
 Reprint. Originally published: Philo, Calif. : Mountain House Press, 1987
 Includes bibliographies.
 ISBN 0-446-38986-2 (U.S.A.)
    0-446-38987-0 (Canada)
 1. Home schooling—United States. I. Colfax, Micki. II. Title.
LC40.C65 1988
649'.68—dc19   88–14721
                                                    CIP

To the Memory of Raj Sookdeosingh
1946–1982

THE SCHOOLBOY

I love to rise in a summer morn,
When the birds sing on every tree;
The distant huntsman winds his horn,
And the sky-lark sings with me.
O! what sweet company.

But to go to school in a summer morn,
O! it drives all joy away;
Under a cruel eye outworn,
The little ones spend the day,
In sighing and dismay.

Ah! then at times I drooping sit,
And spend many an anxious hour,
Nor in my book can I take delight,
Nor sit in learnings bower,
Worn thro' with the dreary shower.

How can the bird that is born for joy,
Sit in a cage and sing.
How can a child when fears annoy,
But droop his tender wing,
And forget his youthful spring.

O! father & mother, if buds are nip'd,
And blossoms blown away,
And if the tender plants are strip'd
Of their joy in the springing day,
By sorrow and cares dismay,

How shall the summer arise in joy
Or the summer fruits appear.
Or how shall we gather what griefs destroy
Or bless the mellowing year,
When the blasts of winter appear.

 —William Blake,
  from SONGS OF EXPERIENCE, 1794

Contents

Acknowledgments

Many friends have contributed to the development of our homeschooling ideas and activities over the years. We are especially grateful to the following, who, contrary to usual practice, we hold collectively responsible for our failures as well as our successes: Bruce and Ling Anderson, Terry Anderson, Bob and Karen Altaras, Angel Arzan, Lew and Janet Baer, Peggy Bates, Jennifer Bice, Chris Bing, Ann Bullwinkel, Norman and JoAnn Charles, Manning and Irene Davis, Jan Dizard, Toby Egeth, Lelia Filiatrault, Jim Gibbons, Rob and Barbara Goodell, Bob and Roxanne Hedges, Bruce Hering, Diane Hering, Lucile Herreid, Eric and Pat Larson, Don and Patti Lipmanson, Kurt Lorenz, Mary Luther, Steve McKay, Virginia Nash, Grace Neill, Nancy Nonnencamp, Joseph Petelle, Judy Pierce, Chuck Ream, Vernon and Charlene Rollins, Robert Salisbury, Steven Schack, Gerd Schroeter, Morris Shepard, Don Sheckler, Will Siegel, Margaret K. Simmons, Ed and Janet Stockwell, Alice Walker, David Walker, Jan Wax, and Michael Winfree.

Introduction

For the last fifteen years we have educated our children at home. Our oldest son, Grant, graduated with high honors from Harvard, and was the recipient of a Fulbright fellowship. His brothers Drew and Reed are presently undergraduates there. Our youngest son, Garth, thirteen, has a few more homeschooling years ahead of him.

When Grant was admitted to Harvard in 1983, his educational experience received widespread attention, and we found ourselves being cast in the role of homeschooling "experts." It was a role we did our best to avoid, in part because we felt that parents did not need yet another set of authorities telling how they should raise their children, and in part because we believed that our experiences—as teachers-turned-ranchers—were so different from those of most parents as to make them of little real value to those who hoped to learn from us.

However, as we talked with hundreds of parents over the next few years, we came to the realization that there was, and continues to be, a need for the exploration of possibilities and a sharing of experiences among parents who want to see their children obtain the best education possible. And when Drew and Reed were admitted to Harvard in 1986 and 1988, we found ourselves increasingly being called upon to tell our story.

Doing that turned out to be a more difficult task than we had envisioned. Our homeschooling program was not derived from a set of neatly-organized principles that guided our day-to-day activities. We did not attempt to implement a particular educational philosophy, but, rather, attempted to respond to the evolving needs of the children more or less in an ad hoc fashion. Because of this, our subsequent efforts to reconstruct and rationalize what was largely a trial-and-error process proved to be a rather complex undertaking. We discovered that our deep-seated aversion to educational ideologies in general, and pop ideologies in particular, made it impossible for us to condense a decade and a half of experience into a few easily-apprehended directives which, if followed, would ensure homeschooling success. The educational experience is simply much too complex, too varied, and too rich to be reduced to a neat formula or two, or a set of pat and trendy phrases.

Rather, it is our intent in the pages that follow to be as concrete as possible and to provide the reader with an account of what we did and how we did it, an abbreviated critique of public education, our assessment of the advantages of homeschooling, and a basic inventory of materials that we found useful over the years.

Some readers may conclude that despite our disclaimers we do in fact have an educational philosophy. If so, it is only that children *will* learn, *will* aspire to excellence, if we recognize and respect their different interests and abilities and give them a chance to develop them. In our view, every child is gifted in one way or another. The tragedy is that this is denied every day, in word and in action, in our schools.

Homeschooling is not a panacea. But for increasing numbers of families it offers a degree of hope and opportunity. *Homeschooling for Excellence* is intended to provide a picture of one family's part in what has emerged as perhaps the most dynamic and creative educational movement in decades. We hope that our account will be of interest and helpful to parents of school-aged children and those who are charged with the task of educating them.

HOMESCHOOLING
FOR
EXCELLENCE

CHAPTER 1

Teaching Our Own

Winter, 1985. It is a dark, rainy morning. David is at his desk in the loft and Drew, seventeen, is busy helping fifteen-year-old Reed with his algebra. Micki is in the kitchen helping Garth, nine, with his writing as she rolls out bread dough.

If the weather clears, the books will be put aside and Reed and Drew will spend the afternoon hauling and stacking firewood while Garth works on the goat pen fence. After dinner Drew will bury himself in a pile of *Sky and Telescope* magazines he borrowed from the county library, and Reed will try to finish that Victor Hugo novel that none of the rest of us has ever gotten through.

It is another typical school day at our rural

homestead where, for a dozen years, we have educated our children at home.

Shortly after moving to our 47 acres on a remote, logged-over mountainside in northern California in 1973, we met a number of parents who were teaching or planning to teach their children at home. For some of us located in the hills, homeschooling was almost unavoidable: distances, snow, landslides, muddy roads, and swollen rivers made it all but impossible to transport children back and forth to the public schools in winter. Distances between neighbors with school-aged children precluded the formation of alternative backwoods schools. And then there were political, religious, and philosophical objections to the local schools: they were too conservative or too liberal, too rigid or too informal, too academic or not academic enough, too fundamentalist or not fundamentalist enough.

For most of us, however, a mixture of philosophy and geography impelled us toward homeschooling. We had moved to the country without giving much thought to how our children would be educated, or where, or by whom, but we were imbued with a spirit of self-reliance, and it was all but inevitable that we would begin thinking and talking about "teaching our own." Educational theory and practice, like other orthodoxies of the late sixties and early seventies, were in a state of flux, with critics of public education such as John Holt, Ivan Illich, and Jonathan Kozol

providing the ideological underpinnings for educational innovation. A little paperback by Hal Bennett, *No
More Public School* (Random House, 1972), had
become something of an underground best seller.
More inspirational than informational, and disarming-
ly low-keyed, it suggested strategies for meeting
curriculum requirements, dealing with hostile school
boards, and teaching children at home "legally or
otherwise."

Once we decided to teach our children at home,
we tried to avoid any confrontation with state or local
authorities. We called ourselves The Mountain School,
registered with the state as a private school, estab-
lished a Mountain School checking account, ordered a
ream of letterhead stationery, and, as required by law,
assembled a file containing daily attendance records,
teacher résumés, and course outlines. Perhaps because our children had never been enrolled in the local
schools, or because we asked nobody for permission to
teach them ourselves (in dealing with the bureaucracies we proceeded in a matter-of-fact way) we
encountered no opposition whatsoever. And of course
it worked to our advantage that the local school
system, which ranked as one of the worst in the state,
was having problems enough with unhappy parents:
its administrators were not inclined to create additional problems for themselves by challenging homeschoolers.

*   *   *

And so we began. In retrospect, we seem to have been almost oblivious to the magnitude of the task we were taking on. Chemistry, trigonometry, and foreign languages were years in the future. The job at hand was to teach the boys—then eight, five, and three—to read and do simple arithmetic, and to get a homestead together. We wrote to a dozen publishers for catalogues and ordered sample copies of books, and after several false starts came across a workbook series of readers that captivated the boys and allowed them to work alone and at their own pace to about a sixth-grade level. Grant, the oldest, finished them in less than two years, as did Drew. Reed, our three-year-old, was well into them at four—he had his older brothers as models—and was an accomplished reader before he was five.

Unfortunately, the reading series, we soon discovered, was unique among texts. Most grade-school-level texts we found badly organized, wooden, and insipid—at best—and after trying several math books, abandoned them all and developed our daily exercise sheets.

Elementary sciences were more easily managed, as we were able to locate a wide variety of non-textbook materials on zoology, botany, astronomy, and physics. On our trips to the city we made it a point to check out the offerings in museum bookstores, as well as the two or three shops which specialized in nature books and materials. At home, our efforts to restore the land, to plant gardens, and to improve our livestock, stimulated interest in biology, chemistry, and, eventually, embryology and genetics. Clearing the badly damaged land provided lessons in ecology, and the construction of a house and outbuildings showed the boys the relevance of seemingly arcane subjects such as geometry. Drew, at seven, understood that the Pythagorean theorem was invaluable in squaring up his sheep shed foundation. Grant, at nine, discovered a Pomo Indian campsite on the ridge and was inspired to delve into North American archaeology, an interest which later broadened into studies of Mayan and Aztec cultures.

Literature posed no problem at all. We read widely and had acquired a sizable library of fiction and nonfiction (with more than a smattering of how-to-do-it books!), which the boys began to explore before they were halfway through their reading workbooks. And the county library, some 30 miles away, was virtually plundered every two weeks when we went to town for supplies. And as the boys' interests grew, we built up a rather comprehensive library of reference books, ranging from a set of encyclopedias, which served as a cornerstone, to standard works on genetics, films, sports, and music.

As time went on, we found the task of home-schooling becoming more difficult in some respects and easier in others. Our early command of the various subjects became less relevant as the boys became more knowledgeable. We had taught English and social sciences, but math and the physical and biological sciences we recalled only dimly, as courses we had taken years ago in college. A few years of Latin and French did not prepare us to teach languages, and we were not inclined to try. An increasingly aggravating problem was the dearth of good advanced textbooks. Most science texts do not lend themselves to home study, and literature and social science texts were found to be remarkably effective in transforming inherently interesting materials into dross. But with college looming ahead for the children, we increasingly felt the need to accommodate our wide-ranging but nevertheless unorthodox program to the rigidly categorical entrance requirements of most of the better schools.

At the same time, however, homeschooling was becoming somewhat easier for us only because Grant's experience had, in effect, cleared a trail for the younger boys. Grant, who had to bear the brunt of our sometimes mistaken choice of texts and other reading materials, knew what had worked and what hadn't, and was able to counsel his younger brothers on what to read, and when, and what to ignore. "Spend a few months on the pre-algebra book," he would tell Drew. "It'll make it easier for you later on." "Don't read Steinbeck for a couple more years," he suggested to Reed, who, at nine, was looking for new authors to

conquer. "You'll appreciate him more when you're a
little older."

    Still, it was not until Grant had run the gauntlet
of college-entrance examinations and did well that we
had any firm evidence that our homeschooling efforts
had, in conventional terms, measured up. Although
we had never doubted the quality of the homeschooling we were providing, we were interested in, if not
terribly concerned about, how the boys would do when
it came time to take the Scholastic Aptitude and
various standard achievement tests. We had emphasized creativity and the pleasures of learning over the
years, and had no evidence—or expectation—that our
approach would provide the boys with an ability to
perform well on what are, after all, for the most part
relatively mindless standardized tests. But of
course—and to our great satisfaction—it did.

    How much of a part did our isolation play in
keeping at homeschooling over the years? Certainly
it played a large part initially, but as time went on
it became less of a factor as we became increasingly
aware of the clear advantages homeschooling offered.
Nevertheless, isolation did play a part. With no
television (the rugged terrain blocked signals) and no
neighbors, we had few distractions. Engaged in the
arduous and time-consuming task of helping their
parents establish a homestead, the boys learned to
value every opportunity to read and study. Time was a

scarce resource, and they quickly learned to use it effectively. Math and grammar might get boring at times, but once those were out of the way, they could look forward to time for other more interesting projects. Each boy carved out an area of specialization. Grant became our livestock expert, Drew the astronomer, Reed the musician-athlete, and Garth our naturalist-artist.

Some have suggested that our success with homeschooling results from our backgrounds as high school and college teachers. Perhaps, but it is not all that apparent to us that our teaching "expertise" has been especially valuable. All parents, after all, are teachers, and it is only the *formal* education of our children that most of us entrust to the "experts." In homeschooling, the children typically teach themselves, with the parents appropriately relegated to the job of suggesting courses of study and being available to answer questions—an uncomplicated process which we discuss in later chapters.

Admittedly, parents who have had teaching experience probably have a clearer idea of *why* they are teaching their children at home, and as a result are probably initially more confident than parents who have had no formal training. Credentials also have the effect of warding off friends, relatives, and officials who feel obliged to monitor and comment on the propriety and effectiveness of teaching one's children at home. There is no question that our teaching credentials (invalid in California, however, though previously accepted in five other states!) made our job easier in this respect. Only an old friend who knew of my long-ago aversion to math questioned my ability to teach it, and it is certain that our years of teaching and research in the schools would have been an asset had a hostile official ever challenged our right or competence to teach our children at home. But more than credentials, experience builds confidence—and the ability to recover from mistakes. Any parent who takes on the job of teaching his or her child at home must be prepared to make mistakes—and occasionally big ones. Several years ago, for example, we were surprised when Grant, who had been good in math up until then, seemed to be having an inordinate amount of trouble with algebra. The fault, as it turned out, was ours, for we had selected a text that was used in a University of California correspondence course without examining it closely, only to discover, belatedly, that it employed the now discredited and abandoned "new math" concepts that were in vogue in the early sixties. By the time that we took Grant's complaints seriously, he had lost, as he became fond of pointing out, several months of work in math. The episode served to remind us—by then, we had been homeschooling for years—that we were indeed capable of making mistakes, and of the need to critically examine texts, however authoritative they might appear. But most importantly, it reinforced our belief that learning will take place if the

child is given appropriate materials and opportunities:
Grant, with a new text, discovered that he did enjoy
math after all, and, eventually, went on to earn A's in
calculus at Harvard.

Of course homeschooling requires a degree of
commitment. Both time and money are required if the
homeschooling effort is to succeed even over the short
run. Cash is a necessary first ingredient. For example,
we spend approximately one hundred dollars a year on
textbooks, and about another two hundred dollars on
other books and materials per child. Our library
represents an outlay of several thousand dollars, and
we have invested over a thousand dollars in laboratory
equipment. And of course there are language tapes,
special events, and music and ceramics lessons to be
paid for. But, fortunately, not all at once. As we
indicate in the chapters that follow, homeschooling
requires relatively little in the way of materials,
provided that they are carefully chosen.
Even in the aggregate, the cash outlays are
insignificant compared to the required investment of
parents' *time*. For even the most self-reliant of
homeschooled children make major demands upon
their parents. Homeschooling parents, like physicians
and veterinarians, are expected to be on call at all
times. And there is homework: David, for example,
has spent dozens of hours poring over math books
ranging from preschool to college level, in search of

suitable texts, and Micki has done the same in pursuit of appropriate English and history materials.

Time, of course, is money, and a parent who forgoes a career or employment opportunity to teach his or her child at home may be making the right decision, but it can be an expensive one. Moreover, some parents simply do not have the luxury of being able to choose between homeschooling and employment outside the home: most single parents, as well as many working women with school-aged children, cannot consider giving up their jobs in order to teach their children at home.

But as a rural family engaged in a collective effort to create an economically viable homestead, and with both of us sharing the teaching, we were able to integrate homeschooling into the day-to-day life of building, clearing, planting, tending, and harvesting. The boys were an integral part of this work from the outset and as such were an asset. Had they been obliged to spend their days in some distant school, it is unlikely that we would have been able—or had the incentive—to develop the homestead as we did. Like farm families of the not-so-distant past, we needed the help of the boys, and homeschooling made that available.

Some have suggested that by teaching our sons at home we are sheltering them from reality. "What's it going to be like when they have to go out into the *real world?"* was the refrain. Grant's performance at Harvard provided an easy, if somewhat misleading answer, for what the question reveals is an inability to comprehend the fact that homeschooling provided our boys with "real world" experiences they would never have encountered in a conventional learning situation. Because they have learned to value and make good use of their time, they have developed skills that most children simply do not have the time or opportunity to acquire.

Many parents—often of very young children— have told us that they plan to teach their children at home when they are older. Few endeavors are more satisfying than helping a child learn to read or do sums. But children, like puppies, grow up, and they can go through some awkward stages. Sometimes the child who was such a delight a half-dozen years earlier can be amazingly obnoxious when he or she is having trouble with chemistry or grammar. But close and constant interaction has its rewards. Parents who complain that they don't understand their teen-aged children bemuse us. Our years as homeschooling parents and children, as teachers and students, have taught us, if anything, the importance of working to understand and support each other to the very fullest extent possible.

It is nearly midnight, and a storm rages outside. We review the day's activities and plan for another rainy day. Garth needs more work in math. Drew and Reed have written essays that David should take a look at in the morning. If it stops raining, we should burn some of those brush piles down the hill. Another day on the homestead, another day of home-schooling.

CHAPTER 2
A Homeschooling
Odyssey

Our children have not been exclusively home-schooled. Only Garth, our youngest, who has never been in a classroom, can claim that distinction. Reed and Drew briefly attended public school, and Grant logged nearly two years in four different schools in three countries by the time he was ten years old. His, our own, and to a lesser extent the younger boys' experiences in some very different educational settings led us to consider—and later strongly reinforced our commitment to—home-schooling.

Unlike many homeschooling parents, we have had rather extensive and varied involvements with schools and educational systems. By the time our children were ready for school in the early seventies, we had devoted more than a dozen years to teaching, researching, and writing about education. Our work in the classroom, as educational consultants, and, later, as parents, provided us with a number of different perspectives on contemporary education and formed our attitudes and approaches to the education of our own children.

Micki had started her teaching career in a suburban high school in 1959, just two years after the ascent of Sputnik, an event that precipitated that era's "crisis" in education. Blame for America's having "fallen behind the Russians" was attributed in large part to the schools. Educators were given a clear mandate to get the nation back in the Cold War race for space, and "educational excellence" was the rallying cry of the day.

It was a time of educational change, one in which teachers were able to take advantage of renewed public and government support for education and encourage innovation and creativity in the classroom. For those in the middle-class suburban schools such as those in which Micki was teaching, this was a good time to be a teacher. One had access to new materials, ideas, and methodologies, and was encouraged to demand the very best, unconstrained by older, now-discredited approaches, from students.

But other forces were at work as well. Even as

teachers were being encouraged to promote creativity
and innovation, the federal government, with the first
of what were to become a near avalanche of mandated
and categorical programs, was beginning to intrude
into historically locally controlled public education.
Within a decade local control of school districts was
transferred, primarily because of changes in patterns
of funding, to state and federal agencies. Sputnik had,
in effect, transformed American education into a
centralized system in which organizational men and
women—administrators and bureaucrats—rather
than teachers and students, became the key players in
a very big, very expensive game. It is a legacy which
haunts and poisons the classroom a generation later.

But in the early sixties we were not concerned
about educational trends. Graduate work took us to
England, where Micki briefly taught in what V. S.
Pritchett calls a "plain government school"—officially,
a "Secondary Modern School." Ostensibly reformed
after World War II to promote equality of opportunity,
English schools nevertheless generally reflected and
reinforced social class divisions. The Secondary Modern Schools warehoused working-class youths who,
having failed the national "Eleven-plus" placement
examination, were tracked into its quasi-vocational
programs. Middle-class families, of course, routinely
bundled their "Eleven-plus failures" off to one of the
many "public"—in fact, private—schools that pre-

dated the postwar educational reforms and historically played such an important part in perpetuating social class distinctions.

Micki's Secondary Modern School, situated in a picturesque, thatched-roof village south of London, didn't pretend to provide serious vocational education, but was rather a genteelly shabby, undemanding sort of place in which the staff understood its job to be that of keeping order until the boys reached the school-leaving age of fourteen and could enter the workforce, begin an apprenticeship, or go on the dole. Courses were of no great importance, and teachers were assigned to them on a more or less haphazard basis. As the newest—and American—recruit, Micki found herself teaching, in the course of a single semester, music, shop, math, history, and English to classrooms of academically demoralized youths. The job was less than inspiring, so when presented with a chance to transfer to a "Comprehensive" school in London, she leaped at the opportunity.

Like the American high schools after which they were vaguely modeled, the Comprehensive schools were designed to serve a wide variety of students, and today might be called "shopping mall schools." But the English attempt to emulate the better features of the American model was constrained by the fact that the more able, ambitious, and affluent English students, in accord with tradition, were sent to the "public schools." As a result, the

Comprehensive schools were not socially inclusive, but rather served, again, a largely lower-middle- and working-class constituency. Part vocational, part general studies, and, to a very limited extent, college-preparatory, they had become, by the early sixties, educational catch-alls, schools in which everything was tried but nothing done very well. And although she did not recognize it as such at the time, Micki was getting a taste of what the American high school was even then in the process of becoming as the federal and state bureaucracies were consolidating their control over public education.

The next few years did not lack for educational variety. Micki taught in suburban Chicago, a New England milltown, and a black school in St. Louis. The results were mixed. Parents might be supportive and students motivated, but with the increased power accorded educational bureaucrats following the passage of the Elementary and Secondary Education Act in the mid-sixties, curriculum, content, and, perhaps most importantly, the teacher's authority and autonomy in the classroom underwent significant transformations. It was becoming increasingly difficult to be a teacher in an era in which uniformity, compliance, and administrative control were in ascendance. And if it was becoming increasingly difficult to be a good teacher, it was clearly more difficult to obtain a first-rate education in the typical American public school.

As a professor of sociology at a state university,

David was in a position to see the effects of deteriorating public education. Bright freshmen who had serious difficulties reading and writing, who could not manage relatively simple concepts, and who were lacking in intellectual curiosity or creativity, were commonplace. Remedial work at this point was seldom effective: the damage had already, and irreparably, been done. David's research interests in education resulted in his being awarded a large grant to study the impact of social structure on school performance, and Micki joined him in conducting the project, which consisted of testing thousands of pupils, interviewing teachers, administrators, and community leaders, and directing surveys of public attitudes toward education. The findings were unexceptional but clear: the schools were doing a poor to fair job of educating most children, and a very bad job of educating the children of the poor. And despite expressed public support for education, community leaders—those in a position to demand and implement educational change—were generally uninformed about educational issues. Where education was on the agenda, the issues were largely divisive, centering upon matters such as teacher militancy, community control, and busing, which for the most part obfuscated, rather than helped clarify basic problems confronting public education. Educational bureaucrats were the prime beneficiaries of what later came to be viewed as a period of educational turmoil: while communities divided along racial and

class lines, state and federal agencies—through legis-
lation and funding—were transforming traditional
state and local relationships. The impact of a public
school monopoly far removed from and virtually
unaccountable to local communities would not be
noted until the early eighties, but by then the bureaucrats would be in a position to successfully resist any
real effort to reform public education.

But in the early seventies our interests had
shifted from educational policy research to the more
immediate and personal task of providing our children
with an education. In the fall of 1971 Grant, like most
six-year-olds, entered the first grade. It was, by all
indicators, a "good school"—well-funded, with small
classes, a heterogeneous student body, an adequate
physical plant, and, presumably, dedicated teachers.
And although we had ample reason to be professional-
ly critical of public schools in general, we had given
relatively little thought to how our children might
function in a classroom setting. But, after all, they
were reasonably bright, and we intended to provide
the kind of home support that is said to ensure school
success.

It took only a week before we began to observe
some changes in Grant. Usually active and voluble, we
noticed that he had become listless and withdrawn. He
assured us it wasn't school—it was "okay." But by the
end of the month, during which his behavior hadn't

improved, he admitted that, yes, it was school. It was "dumb" and "a waste of time." Although not the most articulate of critiques, it was sufficient to prompt us to visit the school.

We found nothing exceptional. The teacher was briskly cheerful and the children well-behaved. It was a well-managed classroom, the kind any principal would be happy to have parents visit. So what was wrong?

We sat there for two hours, trying to see it from the perspective of a six-year-old. True, it was boring. But we weren't six-year-olds, either. The teacher's cheerfulness was a bit forced, but who could blame her? And the carefully controlled discussions were not much different from the ones we remembered from our elementary school days. If Grant found this oppressive, wasn't this something he'd just have to learn to deal with? Life, after all, isn't all fun and games. Part of growing up is learning to deal with regimentation and boredom. Sure, it was a waste of time, but how valuable is a six-year-old's time anyhow?

But however we might try to rationalize it, Grant was right: this was stupid and a waste of time. There was no way we could justify hours in this classroom, no way we could tell him that school was something that had to be endured. Perhaps Grant would have to face dreary reality eventually, but not now. There had to be other options.

* * *

We'd heard about the New City School. It was on the edge of the ghetto in an abandoned high school building, run by a group of maverick teachers. We were wary of the so-called "free" and "alternative" schools of the day, too many of which, we felt, projected some pretty questionable cosmic and educational ideologies in the rhetoric of freedom. A day, and then another, at New City convinced us that it was different. There was an educational philosophy, to be sure—one that suggested, very gently, that education, being, literally, a "drawing out" process, requires only that children be given every opportunity to explore and experiment with ideas and materials as they mature, and that in the process they will acquire higher level conceptual skills. And because all children do not possess the same interests, abilities, or needs, it is important to recognize and encourage individual differences rather than suppress or deny them. It was a perspective that critics would later term "liberationist," but one which we, at least in broad terms, found appealing. And at New City it seemed to work. Teachers did not teach, but were there to provide support and guidance as children worked on their individual projects at their own pace. There was no curriculum, no agenda—only books, science materials, field trips, and a supportive staff.

Grant didn't learn to read or write or do sums that year. He engaged the teachers in long discussions, painted, sculpted, and did natural science projects. Clearly, he was enjoying this school—it was never "dumb" or a "waste of time." We hoped, but were not entirely confident, that he was learning to think.

Some other parents were less hopeful, less confident. What about the basics—reading, writing, and arithmetic? How could you explain to the neighbors or relatives that your seven-year-old who was attending that private school couldn't read or write, and, what was worse, didn't seem to feel any need to learn to do so? Just what did they learn there? What purpose was served by visits to old people's homes, the farmers' market, art galleries, and the riverfront? Wasn't this carrying progressive education a little too far?

It didn't take long. By the end of the year the small group of teachers who had organized the school, who had been more interested in bringing out the best in children than in indulging the misplaced expectations of their parents, were gone as a result of the efforts of some wealthy parents who wanted a more conventional program and staff. By fall New City was transformed into a very conventional, very expensive school. But by then we were in North Africa, waiting for the political situation in Uganda to settle out so David could take up a teaching post at the university in Kampala.

It was to have been a great adventure. David's political sociology had earned him some formidable enemies in his field, and after years of academic politics we needed a change of pace and scene. East Africa, with its people, wildlife, and rugged landscapes, was exotic, and the teaching job at one of the continent's oldest and best universities appealing.

But we were not about to risk our lives for a change of scene. Within days of our arrival in Africa, Uganda's dictator, Idi Amin, launched the first of his murderous assaults on his countrymen, and as the situation worsened, it became clear that this was an especially inopportune time to take up the teaching of politics in that country. To conserve what was left of our rapidly depleting savings, we rented a house in Agadir, a coastal resort town in southern Morocco, where we planned to wait it out, for all indications were that the madman Amin would not remain in power for very long and we could continue on to Uganda in the not-too-distant future.

And so we shopped in the ancient souks, visited the medina, and went on excursions to ruins in the desert. But without books, toys, or friends, the boys were becoming restless. It was time to look for a school.

It was now mid-term and the "European" French school was filled. The only available alternative, we discovered, was a one-room private school located in a drab mud building on the edge of town. The owner and sole teacher, it turned out, was a hefty middle-aged Frenchwoman whose staff consisted of a toothless, grim-faced old man of perhaps eighty whose primary function, we later discovered, was to discipline the students. Neither spoke English, and instruction was in French, but there would be no problem, the teacher assured us, since most of the students spoke Berber at home and didn't know any more French than did our boys—who knew none. Tuition was two dollars a week, paid in advance.

It obviously wasn't the best of situations, and we left Grant and Drew to their care with more than a few misgivings. But at least it would give them something to do, and maybe they'd even learn a little French in the month or so before we headed on to East Africa.

Not Drew. He lasted until noon. Home for lunch, he declared that he wasn't going back. No explanation was forthcoming—he simply wasn't going back. Grant provided the background: Drew had spent the morning with his hands folded on his desk in front of him while the teacher worked with the older students and the old man patrolled the aisles slapping students who dared talk or look around. It was Drew's first experience with organized education, and he was not about to indulge it further.

Grant had fared only a little better. He'd been given what appeared to be an Arabic version of *Dick and Jane* and a notebook, and had been otherwise ignored. It was not an auspicious beginning, and certainly unlike the New City School.

The next day Grant reported that two of his classmates had been dragged to the front of the class and paddled for reasons he didn't understand; they hadn't been acting up in any way, and he suspected that it had something to do with their classwork. And several days later, when Grant was sharply admonished for something about his work, he told us he was worried that he might be next in line for a paddling, since the teacher had snatched his notebook from his desk, waved it at the class, and shook her finger in his face, shouting something in French. This simply wouldn't do; a visit was in order.

The teacher met us at the schoolroom door. Yes, something was wrong, she said. Look at this, she exclaimed, holding up Grant's notebook and pointing to a page on which he had printed some letters. "Look," she shrieked, "Look at this!" When we indicated, as best we could in our fractured French, that we didn't understand the problem—surely his printing, which was acceptable enough by our standards, could not have provoked such fury—she became even more angry. Obviously our son had inherited his bad habits from his doltish parents. Now the old man was beside her, emphatically shaking his head in agreement. We had a trouble-making child and were refusing to admit it.

We looked at each other, backed away, and then turned and retreated across the courtyard as the voices of the teacher and old man followed after us. Safely away, we tried to make some sense of the episode: it was stress or madness.

A week later we were on our way back to America and, soon after, in California. It proved to be the right move: Idi Amin remained in power for another eight years.

Homesteading in the mountains of California's Coastal Range turned out to be at least as interesting, and certainly more demanding than our brief African adventure. For one thing, northern California was wilder than Morocco, if not East Africa. Bear, boar, and mountain lion occasionally visited our ridge, and deer, raccoon, jackrabbit, skunk, and quail were everywhere. And there was no lack of things to do. There was brush—manzanita, oak, and madrone—to be cleared and burned, stumps to be dug out, wood to be milled, a garden to be planted, a road to be put in, and a house to be built. The five of us—Garth was born a couple of years later—worked side by side, doing everything ourselves in an effort to test the limits of our self-sufficiency. We were all novices, young and old, all learning to do things none of us had ever done before. This was better than school, even the New City School; it was a great adventure.

But the adventure had to be interrupted two years later when we came to the sobering realization that if the homestead were ever to become a going concern, we'd need additional capital for improvements. A short-term visiting professorship in Canada beckoned. We packed off to northern Ontario, where Micki substituted in the local high school and the three oldest boys—we'd just adopted Garth—attended school for the last (and in Reed's case, the first) time.

By now, though, they'd been spoiled. In the two years on the land they had learned how to use their time as they saw fit and necessary. They had learned to cherish the hours they were able to spend reading. Now, in school, reading was represented as something of a chore, and the daily regimen of the classroom interfered with what they knew was important. And of course their individual interests were of no consequence here; in school they were expected, compelled, usually for not very good reasons, to respond to the dictates of others. Pointless and time-consuming assignments—clearly busywork—did nothing to improve their opinions of courses or teachers. School simply got in the way of doing worthwhile things. But unlike many other children who have come to the same unremarkable conclusion, their views were endorsed by their parents.

When we returned to the California homestead six months later—and just in time to plant the garden—the boys' school days were clearly behind them. Now that they had had a taste of formal schooling after two years of *real* learning, they could appreciate the difference. There was no question about it now. For better or worse, we were committed to homeschooling.

CHAPTER 3

The Trouble With School

The public education bureaucracy survives—indeed, thrives—today largely because most Americans, including the most critical and, oddly enough, the worst served, support the concept of public education even in the face of an abysmal performance by an institution rife with mediocrity, ineptitude, and political corruption. For many people, the alternatives are inconceivable, unattractive, or unavailable. Private schools, for the most part economically or religiously exclusive, are generally perceived as being the province of special groups or interests, with the result that the vast majority of young people are consigned to what is in fact a public school monopoly, where they are expected to adapt to organizational requirements in the name of education.

Few observers of the current educational scene

29

would deny that American education is in deep trouble. But even fewer of its critics are inclined to attribute the crisis to deep-rooted structural defects or, indeed, essentially fallacious assumptions about the function of public education in America today. Establishment critics—the kind that sit on blue-ribbon panels convened by politicians—have a decidedly vested interest in seeing the perpetuation of public education much along the same lines as presently constituted. Lofty pronouncements about the "rising tide of mediocrity" may briefly attract the attention of the media and fuel endless educational conferences, but do not address basic issues in any meaningful way. This is not surprising, for most panelists would prefer to believe that the remedies are near at hand and need only to be put in place by dedicated administrators, implemented by revitalized teachers, and supported by grateful parents. The real problem, notes Theodore Sizer, is the prevailing assumption that "our schools are basically OK; let's just push them a little harder, add an eighth period to a seven-period day, add thirty days to a 180-day-a-year schedule, test the kids more."* Such "solutions" allow critics to evade the real issues and, indeed, only strengthen the notion that, basically, our schools are all right.

---

*All quotations in this chapter are from "How Not to Fix the Schools," *Harpers* (February 1986), pp. 39–51, and John H. Bunzel, editor, *Challenge to American Schools* (Oxford, 1985).

But even these piecemeal proposals for reform are not likely to be implemented in any meaningful way, says Joseph Adelson. That would take a bitter struggle within educational and political establishments that do not yet comprehend the "debacle of American Schooling in the recent past." The educational establishment, "sluggish" and "defensive," is simply "unwilling to undertake change, unable to grasp the nature of the complaints being made, or too preoccupied with finances and housekeeping to give more than cursory attention to issues of pedagogy."

Not so, counters Walter Karp. Such criticisms of the establishment really miss the point, which is that American schools are doing *precisely* the kind of job political and educational authorities desire. The primary function of public schools, says Karp, is to "habituate students to unfairness, inequality and special privilege." The purpose of education, he argues, is to "prevent citizenship and stifle self-government," to ensure a public that is docile and mindlessly deferential to authority. It is no accident that schools most resemble prisons, he says, and that most Americans "spend their youth becoming accustomed to prison life." But as George Bernard Shaw once wrote, in prison the prisoners are not forced to read books written by the wardens.

Is Karp's characterization overdrawn? Perhaps. Whatever their motives or shortcomings, education and political leaders surely are not *consciously* undemocratic. Albert Shanker, president of the million-member American Federation of Teachers, makes a perhaps more telling point:

> The need to control children, to harbor them for a certain amount of time away from their work or otherwise engaged parents, tends to become *the most important function schools perform*. And this custodial function often conflicts with, even dominates, the others.

Of course Shanker's remarks may be dismissed as little more than an attempt to absolve his constituents—classroom teachers—of responsibility for the deterioration of public education. But the mere fact that teachers can be reasonably described as babysitters says something about the state of the profession. Is it any wonder that they have the highest burn-out and drop-out rate of any major occupational group? It is not surprising that so many teachers choose to become administrators in order to avoid becoming burned-out crowd-control officers.

But of course the problem is not so much one of how teachers are perceived or how they perceive themselves, but that American schools have become, for a variety of good and bad reasons, *industrialized*—centralized, hierarchical, and standardized. And whereas these organizationally "rational" characteristics may be entirely appropriate to the production of automobiles or television sets, they are clearly antithetical to education. In practice, industrialized education means that almost from the moment a child enters school he or she is age-graded, sorted, labeled, and resorted according to currently fashionable criteria. This is assembly-line education, in which the child is processed, over the years, much like a can of soup or a piece of hardware.

Educators must, of course, deny this, and will seize upon virtually any opportunity to publicly declare their undivided attention and devotion to the "needs of the children." But in reality, their primary objective is that of moving the product—schoolchildren—on down the line with a minimum of interference from subordinates, parents, the public, or the children themselves. Control is paramount, while subservience and conformity are valued and rewarded. Ends are transformed as education is reduced to an incidental—if occasionally troublesome—element in the day-to-day operations of the organization. Education is neglected as organizational needs are given precedence over those of the individual. But to attempt seriously to address such issues is to take on a thankless task. A dozen years ago several "radical" educators proposed a number of widely publicized ideas to revitalize American education, on the assumption that educational change was both desirable and possible. But few of these were implemented, and even fewer survived, and most of these critics have gone on to other things, and have left the field of educational reform to the functionaries who advise and staff the variously convened educational commissions and panels, which are generally unremarkable except for the banality of their recommendations— greater teacher participation in decision-making, performance funding, and school district reorganization—none of which addresses the underlying, organizational and philosophical defects of contemporary assembly-line education.

Is there a way out? Not as long as the educational establishment and its political allies are in a position to massively resist any serious effort to break up the public school monopoly. The sad prospect is that American public schools are not going to change very much at all over the next decade or two, short of some unlikely social or political upheaval. Parents who are concerned about their children's education would accordingly do well to view official promises of change with considerable skepticism and search out alternatives instead. Obviously there is a need to expose the faults of public education and to work for genuine change. But parents have a more immediate obligation to do everything possible to ensure that their children obtain an education that will enable them to develop to the fullest of their abilities. It is not an impossible undertaking, but one that requires that they not be distracted, courted, intimidated, or co-opted by educational authorities or well-meaning but ineffectual reformers who are, perhaps inadvertently, helping to perpetuate a fundamentally untenable set of educational arrangements presided over by a public school monopoly.

CHAPTER 4

The Homeschooling Alternative

If public education is, as one critic asserts, "a briar patch of ineptitude, stubbornness, and entrenched interests" and "best left alone," what are the alternatives? Homeschooling is just one—an individual solution to a general problem. It provides few if any answers to the important question of just how American education can be seriously reformed or transformed. Certainly, keeping children out of school is a clear vote of no-confidence in public education, but even as thousands of parents choose, perhaps reluctantly, this alternative, it will not have much of an impact on American education in general. Homeschooling is unlikely to have any immediately discernible effect upon many of the nation's sixteen thousand school districts, excite very many of its three million teachers, dislodge any of the tens of thousands of school functionaries, or, most discouragingly of all, make classroom life any more meaningful for the millions of children whose parents cannot or will not take them out of the assembly-line schools. Homeschooling is an individual response to what increasing numbers of parents see as an educational system that fails to serve the needs of their children.

But of course homeschooling is not all of a piece. It is characterized by considerable variety in content and style. Some parents commit themselves and their children to homeschooling almost from the moment the children are born, others drift into it, and still others consider it years after their children are having trouble in school.

Some teach their children at home for very clearly defined political, religious, philosophical, or pedagogical reasons, while others—perhaps even a majority—would be hard-pressed to say why, exactly, they teach their children at home. Some parents see homeschooling as a short-term solution to a temporary problem, while others are committed to homeschooling over the long term. Some teach their children at home because of what *is* being taught in the schools, while others choose to homeschool because of what is *not* being taught. There are those who teach their children at home because the schools are too rigid, while others do so because the schools are not structured to their liking. And some regard homeschooling as a radical action, while others see it as an essentially conservative undertaking.

Homeschooling parents have variously criticized the public schools for any number of shortcomings—for promoting anti-intellectualism, conformity, and passivity, for rigidity and for disorganization, for over-socializing and for under-socializing, for testing too often and for testing too little, for tracking and for failing to acknowledge differences, and for course content of every variety. Homeschooling, in short, is a very mixed bag, and provides a wide variety of examples for parents who are, or are considering, educating their children at home.

Homeschoolers, whatever their motives or orientations, will agree that their approach to education is superior to other alternatives in at least four areas. Homeschooling, unlike other options, allows parents and children to exercise *control*—over content, methods, timing, and personnel. Second, it is *more efficient* than most other forms of formal education. Third, it encourages *autonomy*, and finally, it promotes *creativity*.

Each of these, of course, has different weight from home to home and from child to child, but in sum they compromise the fundamental rationale for homeschooling.

CONTROL OVER CONTENT

Although most aren't unduly concerned about it, parents who send their children to others to be taught relinquish control over what their children will be taught, and when. Most people—and especially professional educators—presume that there is, indeed, a body of knowledge to which children must be systematically exposed as they progress through the grades. But closer examination of this notion reveals that it is more of an organizational housekeeping consideration than a pedagogically sound concept. The public school curriculum—which embodies, at least theoretically, *what* is to be learned and *when*—is in fact nothing more than a hodgepodge of materials and assumptions resulting from the historical interplay of educational theories, political expedience, education fads and fashions, pretensions to culture, demagoguery, and demography. It is by no means, as the professional educators would have it, a coherent "course of study" or, as the more pretentious among them would have it, a "distillation of our common culture." Rather, as devised and enforced by government bureaucracies over recent years, the curriculum inflicted upon public school children has come to resemble *dogma*—"doctrines put forward by some authority, especially a Church, to be accepted as true without question."*

Of course even the most casual review of almost any elementary or high school curriculum will reveal just how arbitrary—which is to say, irrational—it is in its age-grading and categorization of knowledge. But because the curriculum is devised by "specialists" who are presumed, at least within the ranks of the educational bureaucracy, to know just what should be taught and when, the notion that learning is a top-down, externally imposed process, a "laying-on of culture," is perpetuated and reinforced, unchallenged, daily. It is not parents and children who devise the curriculum, who determine what they need to know and when, but the experts who prepackage knowledge and dispense it on schedules of their own devising to children who are treated as if they were to be filled, labeled, crated, and shipped out—all according to some distant authority's work order.

The result is that the classroom teacher's freedom to deal with individual differences is sharply limited. This curriculum-imposed suppression of individual differences is one of the most unfortunate consequences of contemporary assembly-line schooling, for if there is anything that early childhood

Oxford American Dictionary (Avon, 1980).

educational research has contributed to our knowledge, it is that children mature at very different rates,
have very different aptitudes, and vary dramatically
in their ability to put information into meaningful
contexts. A young John Updike may be ready to write
short stories at ten and never develop an interest in
nuclear physics, while a young Linus Pauling might be
inclined in precisely the opposite direction. But in the
public school context, a "good" student is too often one
who fits or is able to adapt to curricular stereotypes,
learning *what* is given *when* it is given. And if the
typical curriculum is to be believed, a good student
will learn the "meaning of Mother's Day" in grades one
and three, about Canada and Mexico in the sixth
grade, to read the newspaper in the tenth (!) grade,
and do nuclear physics in the twelfth.* Even on the
face of it the ordering is absurd, yet such arrangements serve a larger purpose—the need for organizational control and order.

What most educationists refuse to acknowledge
is that real learning, in and out of the classroom,
varies along community, cultural, and class lines, and
from place to place and from era to era. For the most

---

*See William H. Nault, *Typical Course of Study* (World Book,
1980). E. D. Hirsch, Jr.'s best-selling *Cultural Literacy: What
Every American Needs to Know* (Houghton Mifflin, 1987) at-
tempts—unsuccessfully—to parlay the "common culture" assumption into a full-blown theory.

part any standardized, official curriculum is largely meaningless, incoherent, and irrelevant to the lives of most children. It is rather a control mechanism, one which interferes with and undermines education.

But even if it is granted that the typical school curriculum has its faults, can *parents* be trusted to decide what their children will learn? Why not? Clearly, despite the efforts of various experts, committees, panels, and mandates of all kinds, the public schools are failing to impart even the rudiments of learning—reading, writing, and mathematics. In contrast, parents who have assumed the task of educating their children at home have been almost without exception successful in imparting these skills.

And of course once a child has mastered the basics, anything and everything is possible. From that point on parents can custom-fit courses to the interests, needs, and abilities of the child. In a way, public schools do much the same thing for *groups* of students: not everybody takes auto shop or physics or honors courses. Ostensibly, students are grouped according to performance, abilities, and interests, but, in reality, they are segregated primarily in response to organizational needs.

In short, homeschooling parents can ignore what are for the most part government directives as to what shall be taught and when. Rather, parents and children can work together to develop courses of study that address immediate and long-term needs, interests, and capabilities in the context of what they, and not a bureaucracy of decidedly dubious credibility, deem important and necessary.

CONTROL OVER METHODS

Although control over what is taught and when may be the prime concern of most homeschooling parents, *how* children are taught is of equal concern to many. Homeschooling permits parents to choose from a wide variety of methods of teaching, to use and adapt those that work best with their children, and to vary techniques as circumstances demand. This is an important consideration simply because, as most of us know, there is no "best" method of teaching reading, writing, arithmetic—or creative writing or nuclear chemistry. Fashions in teaching change from year to year, from decade to decade, and from generation to generation. The methodological orthodoxy of one era's experts often becomes the heresy of the next. Today's reading experts, for example, are not very well positioned to pontificate about "best" and "correct" methods of teaching reading for the simple reason that their track record in recent years is not very impressive. Similarly, mathematics teachers are appropriately reluctant to advocate currently fashionable methods of teaching math in light of their disastrous endorsement of the now thoroughly discredited "new math" some years ago.

Unlike teachers and administrators, who sometimes seem to have a trained susceptibility to commercially promoted educational gimmickry, parents can be skeptically eclectic in their choice of and commitment to methods and materials. They can continually seek out, sample, test, and discard or retain methods and materials of all kinds without having to worry about professional orthodoxies, fads, or fashions. The art of teaching requires nothing less.

CONTROL OVER TIMING

It seems obvious, yet its implications are almost universally ignored: children learn best when they are intellectually, emotionally, and socially *ready* to learn. And because children are not universally *ready* when age-grade oriented teachers are, learning often does not take place when and as it should. Homeschooling allows parents to regulate the flow of information, the timing of what is taught and when, simply because they, unlike even the most conscientious of classroom teachers, are uniquely positioned to know when their children are and are not ready for various materials. The attentive homeschooling parent is thus able to recognize when to challenge and when to ease up, when to move forward and when to back up for review.

CONTROL OVER PERSONNEL

Most parents have little control over who teaches their children who attend public school; it is usually simply the luck of the draw that decides whether a child will get a good, bad, or indifferent teacher. Occasionally, if a teacher is blatantly incompetent and parents are sufficiently aggressive, a child may be transferred—and leave behind the children of less forceful parents. And because every school system has its incompetents—classroom teachers with serious intellectual, personality, or character defects are not as uncommon as school administrators would like to believe—it is the rare child who manages to progress through twelve or thirteen years of school without having to deal with one or another. Obviously such individuals should not be permitted to remain in the classroom, but incompetent and even abusive teachers, often protected by tenure or publicity-shy administrators, are notoriously hard to dislodge.*

Homeschooling parents may not be the most experienced or patient of teachers, but they are not

---

*For example, in a report by Elaine Herscher, "How Teacher Stress Can Lead to Abuse," *San Francisco Chronicle*, Feb. 11, 1987, school officials acknowledge that abusive teachers are a greater problem than is generally recognized.

likely to find the task so stressful as to become abusive, as have, apparently, too large a minority of public school teachers.

EFFICIENCY

Although one may question the merits of parental control over course content, teaching methods, age-graded education, and staffing, there is no question but that homeschooling is dramatically more *efficient* than public education.

The numbers are straightforward and irrefutable. The child who attends public school typically spends approximately 1,100 hours a year there, but only twenty percent of these—220—are spent, as the educators say, "on task." Nearly 900 hours, or eighty percent, are squandered on what are essentially organizational matters.

In contrast, the homeschooled child who spends only two hours a day, seven days a week, year-round, on basics alone, logs over *three times* as many hours "on-task" in a given year than does his public school counterpart. Moreover, unlike the public school child, whose day is largely taken up by non-task activities, the homeschooled child has ample time left each day to take part in other activities—athletics, art, history, etc.—without having to sacrifice other interests, as is commonly the case in school where, for example, one may have to choose between playing sports or playing in the orchestra simply because of time constraints.

AUTONOMY

The idea that some—perhaps most—children are able to master in a matter of months what is ordinarily spread over several years in school is, to some, an unsettling notion. If true, it means that literally thousands of hours of childhood, if not taken up with school, would have to be filled with something else. Most children, of course, adapt, in varying degrees, to the pace set in school, and are rarely given an opportunity to decide how they would prefer to occupy their classroom hours. The homeschooled child, in contrast, can be given the opportunity to develop projects of his or her own choosing, to invest large blocks of time in undertakings that would be all but unimaginable in school, and, in short, take responsibility for his or her own education.

In a period in which educational "reformers" of the "more is better" variety are calling for longer school days and a longer school year in a desperate effort to respond to the current educational crisis, any suggestion that children might do better if they spent *fewer* hours in school and were given time to pursue their own, *real* interests, is not likely to be taken very seriously, whatever the merits of the idea.

But homeschooled children are given precisely that opportunity. Work can be speeded up or slowed down, and studies put aside for travel or special events as the occasions arise. Unconstrained by an overly long school day, the homeschooled child can become educationally autonomous, as it were, and capable of dealing with learning not as something "out there" and "run by them," as commonly understood, but as an integral part of everyday life, something for which one has to take responsibility.

CREATIVITY

If only by virtue of the freedom it affords, homeschooling promotes creativity. It is an almost inevitable consequence of a program in which self-directed boys and girls are encouraged—and given space—to devise their own programs, to explore, and to experiment at their own pace. It is a topic to which we return again and again in the pages that follow.

All photographs by David and Micki Colfax

CATCHING
THE
SUN

CHAPTER 5
Before Basics

According to child development specialists, most children learn nearly half of all they will *ever* learn by the time they are four or five years old. In view of that, it is remarkable that parents—those who have been primarily responsible for their children's growth over those early, learning-crammed years—can be made to feel somehow inadequate to the task of educating them as they grow older. The widespread acceptance of the notion that parents become incapable of looking out for their children's interests and education once they reach the age of six or seven is perhaps a carryover from an earlier time, when many parents were illiterate or immigrants who themselves lacked the skills their children would need to function in modern industrial society. But today most parents possess the ability to teach their own children, and to do a better job of it than individuals whose credentials typically consist of a degree or two from a lowly education department in a college of no particular distinction, and whose most redeeming attribute is often the ability to find work in any of several thousand bloated school districts.

Most parents, we contend, are more than capable of providing their children with a better education than they could obtain elsewhere. All that is necessary are appropriate learning materials and opportunities, on the one hand, and a nurturing environment, on the other.

Parents will have little trouble understanding what we mean when we talk about the need to provide a nurturing environment. But what are "appropriate learning materials and opportunities"? They are virtually infinite in their variety, and will vary with the age, needs, interests, and abilities of the child. For a sixteen-year-old, they may be woodworking tools, a week of fieldwork at a wildlife refuge, laboratory materials, or a part-time job. For a ten-year-old, a trip to the zoo or a new magazine subscription. And for a five-year-old, good toys.

Toys are not always given proper credit for the part they play in the social, intellectual, and physical development of the child. Perhaps this is because we realize that their contribution is often less than positive.* It is probably harder to find good toys than good children's books: one needs only to visit a chain toy store or tune in to a Saturday morning television show to see just how debased the toy industry has become, and how egregiously it distorts and trivializes the world.

Of course there are some perennial classics which do not merit such an indictment—honest toys such as Tinkertoys, Legos, Lincoln Logs, and, more recently, Fischer Techniks—and which stimulate the imagination and help develop motor skills. Unfortunately, there is an apparent lack of widespread parental interest in efforts to systematically evaluate toys—a Rodale periodical which attempted to do just that suspended publication after just one issue—but parents may find Sally Goldberg's *Teaching with Toys* and *Growing with Games* (University of Michigan Press, 1985) valuable for children up to three years of age, and for three- to six-year-olds, respectively.

Some of the best toys do not come from toy stores. What adult doesn't remember a favorite toy— a boat or a doll—made from scraps of wood or fabric? Parents should not overlook establishments such as craft shops, art suppliers, hardware stores, nurseries, and lumber yards, as sources of play materials. Often bits and pieces—such as wood scraps, fabric remnants, and even old engine parts—gathered from such

*See Brian Sutton-Smith, *Toys as Culture* (Gardner, 1986).

places lend themselves to far more creative uses than most commercially produced toys. One of Drew's all-time favorite Christmas gifts, for example, was a crate full of six-inch-long three-quarter-inch galvanized pipes and assorted connectors, els, and tees, that we had obtained at a building supply house for him when he was four. They didn't allow as many design variations as his Tinkertoys or Legos, but were all the more treasured because of their inherent authenticity—they were "real." It taught us an important lesson: "real things"—tools, building materials, musical instruments, art supplies, and such—have a greater appeal to children than do the various kits and miniaturizations that are so frequently given to them simply because it is assumed that children are unable to appreciate or use the genuine article.

But it is not enough to provide toys—even good ones. There is a world out there—beyond the home and the neighborhood—of museums, libraries, parks, concert halls, factories, markets, construction sites, farms, and fairs, to which the child can be introduced at an early age. It is a world at once more challenging and more complex than the one presented on television or in books, and one to which he or she should be gently, thoughtfully, introduced. Young children cannot be expected to immediately appreciate Picasso or Mozart any more than the fine points of a well-pitched baseball game, and a light touch is usually in order, especially where "culture" is concerned. Children

should not be culturally indoctrinated by well-meaning
but heavy-handed parents any more than by insensi-
tive classroom teachers. Homeschoolers need to take
care not to overwhelm their children with elaborate
"meaningful experiences," for didacticism can be as
antithetical to education in a museum or zoo as in the
classroom. After all, the purpose of exposure is to
encourage growth, and certainly not to inoculate
against the expansion and development of interests.

And interests will emerge, though not necessarily on schedule or in forms parents intend or
expect. A visit to the ballet may result in an aversion
to, instead of an interest in, dance. And budding
artists have been known to prefer baseball to art
galleries. But, more typically, days at the zoo may
evoke a general interest in wildlife, or a special
interest in snakes, or spiders, or bears. Some of these
early interests will be mercifully short-lived, while
others will persist and expand. It is the parents' task
to facilitate the development of these interests to the
point that the child can take control and manage
activities related to them on his or her own.

Natural science projects are especially valuable. They can range from a three-year-old's manage-
ment of an ant farm to a five-year-old's bug collection
or responsibility for the care and feeding of the family
dog or cat. A child who plants and tends even the
smallest garden—and virtually every home has or is
near a place where this can be done—will perhaps

learn more about natural processes and the connected-
ness of diligence, chance, and results than in almost
any other way. Early hands-on experience of this kind
teaches, perhaps better than anything else, the importance of patience, perseverance, and skills.

Good projects inspire, challenge, and build
confidence, but because it is the rare undertaking that
provides these in equal measure, a variety of interests
and activities needs to be encouraged from an early
age. Most—perhaps all—of these may be left behind
as the child matures, but their impact—the development of attitudes and behaviors that will serve
them later in life—will endure.

Real-life, hands-on experience may be all well
and good, but shouldn't the child be encouraged to
learn to read and write as early as possible? Isn't this
at least as important as visiting a museum or planting
a garden? Perhaps not. The notion that children are
given a leg-up on life if they learn to read when very
young was for many years one of the key assumptions
underlying perhaps the most universally-approved of
the federal poverty programs, Head Start, and is
reflected in much of children's educational television
broadcasting. But in fact, there is no evidence that the
acquisition of reading skills at an early age is directly
related to later intellectual attainment. Rather, the
evidence is that reading "head-starts" tend to fade as
other social and psychological factors come into play
as children mature. Indeed, there is evidence that

elementary schoolteachers' preoccupation with teaching reading and writing to five- and six-year-olds may do more harm than good, as many children simply are not "reading ready" at this age.

Parents would do better, it appears, not to concern themselves with the acquisition of reading skills, but to endeavor to provide their children with an *appreciation for reading*. The child who is exposed to books at an early age, who sees his or her parents reading, who is read to, and who is encouraged to spend time with picture books, will all but certainly become a reader in due course. How and when this occurs will vary from child to child and from family to family. Some children, sometimes to the distress of their parents, will be happy to be read to and to look at picture books well past the point at which they would "normally" be reading. Grant, our oldest son, was a late reader. We had moved to the country at about the time when, if in school, he would have been taught to read, and it was a great adventure. Learning to read simply wasn't important. Not until he was nine, and found that his desire to know more about the Pomo Indians who once camped on our ridge required that he learn to read, did he bother to do so. Thus motivated, he was reading college-level anthropology monographs within a year, and was writing short stories based upon his reading.

Reed, in contrast, learned to read at four, partly because he had his older brothers, themselves just learning to read, as role models, and, as we only later realized, partly because he was too young to take part in many of the homesteading activities that occupied so much of their time, and recognized that learning to read would put him on an equal footing with them in at least one area. And Drew and Garth, for no discernible reason, learned to read at the "normal" ages of six and seven, and seem no better or worse for the experience than their divergently different brothers.

The best way to foster an appreciation of reading is to read aloud to young children. Start early with picture books and move on to more challenging materials later, says Jim Trelease, author of the *Read Aloud Handbook* (Penguin, 1985), which, along with Nancy Larrick's *A Parents' Guide to Children's Reading* (Bantam, 1982), provides a comprehensive overview of some of the best of the more than *40,000* children's books now in print.

Of course there is no reason to slavishly work one's way through even the most authoritative list of "treasures" or "classics." It is far better for parents and children to work together, over time, to select books that look interesting, to learn to discriminate between good and bad. But there are some 2,500 children's books published each year, and there is no way even the most industrious family can review more than a small fraction of them. Help is available: the *New York Times*, which publishes a review of children's books each November, and the *Bulletin of the Children's Book Center* (University of Chicago) which reviews some seventy-five new books for children each month, are available in many public libraries or can be obtained directly. But perhaps better still are regular visits to the library, where a couple of hours browsing through new arrivals, talking with librarians about what looks good and not so good, and keeping one's eye out for new books by consistently appealing writers—our favorites were and are Bill Peet, Dr. Seuss, Judith Viorst, Peggy Parrish, and David Macaulay—help to develop habits conducive to learning to read later on. And this—acquiring a degree of familiarity and becoming comfortable with books—is far more important than becoming an early reader who finds no joy in it.

High-quality toys, field trips, and books are the essentials of effective early education. But what about that most ubiquitous of presences, *television*? How can it be articulated with a homeschooling program? Unfortunately, not very readily. Most homeschoolers have to come to terms at some point or other with what someone has called this "monster in every home," and for many this is not easy to do. And there is ample reason for concern. Contrary to the high hopes once held out for it, contemporary television exerts a largely pernicious influence on the lives of American children. Neil Postman, one of the most thoughtful of critics, attributes this to what he calls television's relentless "second curriculum"—its flashy, immediate, and utterly undemanding programming— which he believes seriously undermines children's ability to intelligently comprehend and cope with the real world.*

Paul Cooperman is less sweeping, but no less critical as he observes that a child spends more time between the ages of five and eighteen in front of the television set (15,000 hours) than in school (11,500 hours), and remarks,

> Consider what a child misses during the 15,000 hours he spends in front of the TV screen. He is not working in the garage . . . or in the garden . . . not doing homework, or reading, or collecting stamps . . . not cleaning his room, washing the supper dishes or cutting the lawn . . . not playing baseball or going fishing or painting pictures. Exactly what does television offer that is so valuable that it can replace all of these activities?**

In short, television is an enormous childhood energy drain. But once a parent recognizes this, what

---

*Neil Postman, *Amusing Ourselves to Death* (Viking, 1985), and *Teaching as a Conserving Activity* (Delacorte, 1979).
**The Literacy Hoax* (Morrow, 1982).

can be done? Some—a very few—keep television out
of the home until their children are mature enough to
distinguish between the occasionally worthwhile program and more typical fare. But many parents are
themselves regular viewers, if not addicts, and find it
difficult to impose restrictions on their children in light
of their own habits. One solution is to undergo a
program of gradual withdrawal in which both parents
and children participate. By sharply limiting viewing
to programs carefully selected in advance, parents and
children can *jointly* transform television from a habit
into just one of many activities in which they can
individually or collectively participate.

CHAPTER 6

Tools for Learning

I t is true that a child can be homeschooled without much in the way of specially obtained materials. Most of what is needed can be homemade or borrowed. Certainly public school officials don't allocate much in the way of funds to learning materials: less than five cents out of every education dollar goes for books and supplies.

But no matter how good the local library or how rich in resources a community might be, there are a few, fairly obvious materials that homeschooling— indeed, all—parents might well consider purchasing at some point in order to provide their children with a home environment that is conducive to learning. For children to become more and more independent and educationally self-sufficient as they grow older, resources such as a good home library, art supplies,

musical instruments, laboratory equipment, and hardware of various kinds facilitate exploration, creativity,
and autonomy.

Parents who have embarked upon a reading-
aloud program as suggested in the previous chapter
will have acquired at least a few favorite books. These
are the nucleus of what should become an ever-
expanding home library—that most important collection of tools for learning. More than "children's books"
should be included in the library early on, so that the
read-to-aloud child can begin to understand that books
are tools as well as sources of entertainment. One
needs not to load up on the classics or basic reference
volumes when the child is very young, but the process
of building a good library should not be left too far into
the future, either.

Because a child of four or five is quite capable of
browsing through and being comfortable with a well-
illustrated encyclopedia volume or two, we suggest
that a multi-volume set be made the centerpiece of
every home library. Not any old set will do, and most
emphatically not those antique volumes Aunt Harriet
willed to the family, or the kind you can pick up, a
volume at a time, at the supermarket. Rather, parents
would do well to invest in an attractive and up-to-date
set that the child learns to use and use hard—knocked
around, carried into the bathroom, and read at meals
and in the backyard as well as at the desk. The real
test of an encyclopedia is not how nice it looks up there

on a shelf or what learned authorities have endorsed it, but how much it is used. Even very young children will pick up and spend hours with encyclopedias such as *World Book* and *Compton's* simply because they are so colorful and well-designed, but older children and adults will also find them engaging and informative. Of course they are expensive, but at a time when paperback mysteries go for five or six dollars, twenty dollars per substantial volume is indeed a bargain. Still, some parents may want to consider purchasing a used set that has been updated with annual supplements. In some cities there are bookstores that specialize in used sets at reasonable prices. But first consult Kenneth Kister's *Encyclopedia Buying Guide* (Bowker, 1981), which is available in most libraries, and take a look at the sets there, as each has its special qualities and quirks.

The "children's encyclopedias"—*Childcraft* and *The Book of Knowledge* are the best known—may appeal to parents of young children. Though worthwhile, they are soon outgrown, and those on a limited budget might better invest in a more extensive mix of children's books from a variety of sources.

Next, add some standard—and not so standard—reference books. The *Golden Nature Books* are a good starting point, as they are remarkably inexpensive, colorful, and informative. Follow a few of these with a dictionary or two—a big one for fine points and a smaller one for quick reference, a world atlas, an almanac, and perhaps some specialized sports, music, or art references. A basic reference library should serve the family's interests and, like the encyclopedia, is there to be used. Our reference library* is by no means meant to be "definitive," but rather reflects our interests and idiosyncrasies, as any good family library should.

If possible, build up a wide-ranging library of fiction and nonfiction—obscure as well as best-selling novels, mysteries, how-to-do-its, art and photography books, classics of all genres. Many of these can be picked up at used bookstores for next to nothing. Annual library sales are another especially good place to obtain books at reasonable prices, as are the various publishers' clearinghouses and remainder tables.

Of course, children should be made an integral part of the library-building process from an early age. They should be encouraged to join in searches of old bookstores and in visits to libraries, where they should be permitted to check out even unreasonably large numbers of books to be sorted out at home, a process which teaches the importance of being able to discriminate among the great, the good, the mediocre, and the bad. It is important that children come to regard books as "user-friendly," as tools to be used, rather than venerable artifacts. Hard use, not rever-

*See Appendix 1.

ence, should be encouraged; appreciation of fine and first editions can be acquired later.

As the home library is being assembled, parents will find that books that they feel are important are being rejected by their children. Though disconcerting, at least initially, it should be viewed as evidence that the children are developing tastes and interests of their own—and something that should be encouraged. What this means, of course, is that books that parents remember as classics may sit unread, while others of no apparent value are devoured. And books that one child finds absolutely enthralling may be of no interest whatsoever to another. For this reason we feel that we cannot overemphasize the importance of exposing children—especially when they are young—to as wide a range of books as possible. There are, after all, thousands of books that by one standard or another could be validly termed "classics," and few adults, much less children, ever manage to read more than a tiny fraction of even the very best of these. The goal should not be to "lay on" a preconceived "cultural heritage," whatever that may be, but to allow the child to become a discriminating reader who is capable of making informed and intelligent choices on his or her own terms.

The proliferation of special-interest periodicals in recent years provides the homeschooling family with another rich source of learning materials. Perennial favorites such as *Cricket* and *Highlights for*

*Children** will appeal to younger children, but as interests become more focused they should be encouraged to subscribe—or have friends or relatives give gift subscriptions on holidays or birthdays—to more specialized magazines. *Runner's World, Astronomy,* and *The New Yorker* are favorites around our house today, but just a few years ago the list was very different. Subscriptions, after all, needn't be long-term commitments; as interests change, so should they.

Some of the more generally useful learning tools we've acquired over the years include a variety of typewriters, a good microscope, art and drafting materials, laboratory equipment, and, most recently, a computer. Perhaps the most basic of these is the typewriter. Typewriting is a too-often-underrated skill, but in this age of electronics, when one is all but certain to have to interface with a computer at some point or another, keyboard competence takes on special significance. Unfortunately, as our children's handwriting attests, the early acquisition of typing skills may result in the neglect of "penmanship," but we console ourselves with claims that there is little correlation between academic achievement and the ability to form Palmer-perfect ovals. Most children, if given the opportunity, become enthusiastic typists.

---

*See Appendix 2.

We've used James W. Miller's *Introductory and Personal Typewriting* (Pitman, 1975), but almost any high school manual can be used by ten-year-olds with just a little help from parents.

We've used, returned, and worn out a variety of manual, electric, and electronic standard and portable typewriters over the years and have come to the conclusion that it is probably best to start the young typist out on a sturdy, not-too-complicated manual so as not to intimidate him or her. Later, depending upon use and interest, more sophisticated models can be checked out. We've made it something of a tradition to give each of the boys a state-of-the-art portable at the age of twelve—a tradition that is not likely to persevere in an era of increasingly affordable word-processors.

Even in the home in which there is little talent for or interest in art, a few basic items are desirable. There are always posters to be drawn, cards to be illustrated, and crafts to be decorated, if not paintings to be painted or sculptures to be sculpted. A drawing board, T-square, triangles, and rulers take care of most drafting needs, and a few bottles of acrylic paints will make do for most purposes. More substantial interests should be encouraged with professional-quality materials which, surprisingly, are generally quite reasonably priced, as a visit to an art supply store which, ideally, serves art school students will confirm.

Finally, even though they are expensive and even a bit specialized, a good microscope is invaluable in opening the world of the unseen to young eyes. We recommend a Bausch and Lomb in the three- to four-hundred-dollar range; cheaper models are virtually useless. What makes the microscope an especially valuable learning device is that there are a number of very good books on its use available.*

*See Appendix 3.

CHAPTER 7

The Three R's

Achild who has been read to, who has been exposed to books, and who has been provided with the kinds of support and experiences discussed earlier will almost certainly learn to read and write with relatively little effort. But, some will ask, When? It is a question that will not bother homeschooling parents who understand that children mature at different rates and have different talents and interests that affect "reading-readiness." The only question that needs to concern homeschoolers is, What are the best materials that I can use to teach my child reading, writing, and math skills efficiently and as painlessly as possible?

After years of reviewing materials of all kinds that have been brought to our attention by publishers, educators, and other homeschoolers and variously described as unique, innovative, and creative, we find that (1) most of the early reading and early math products are overpriced, gimmicky, and of relatively little value, (2) reading, writing, and arithmetic workbooks are designed to meet classroom and teacher needs rather than the needs of children, and as such are more concerned with occupying time than with providing real skills in an efficient manner, (3) far less time and effort are needed to provide children with the basics than educators and schoolbook publishers are inclined to admit, and (4) a few readily available books and projects will ordinarily suffice to provide the child with a firm grounding in the basics that will, in turn, allow him or her to get on with the business of higher-order learning and thinking. In short, it is not as lengthy or as complex a process as those with a vested interest in stretching it out and obfuscating it would have us believe.

READING

Of all the materials available to homeschooling parents, few are as valuable as the set of reading workbooks produced by the Sullivan Associates. Conceived by a maverick college professor who was concerned about student reading problems, the *Sullivan Readers* have been developed and tested over the years, and have succeeded in teaching thousands to read—and enjoy it. The workbooks—there are twenty-three of them—carry the reader forward from the adventures of Sam and Ann and Mr. and Mrs. Roundabout through the Greek myths. Part of their appeal is that, unlike most readers, they are engagingly wry, witty, multiracial, and nonsexist.*

Grant began the *Sullivan Readers* when he was nine, and raced through all the workbooks in a year and was soon into adult literature. Each of the other boys proceeded at his own, more leisurely, pace, and by the time the twenty-three workbooks were completed, was fully competent to tackle high school texts, novels, and general nonfiction.

The current Third Edition of the Sullivan Programmed Reading Series is considerably, and, for homeschoolers, unnecessarily more elaborate than the one which captured our attention. Its components range from "Reading-Readiness Lists" to filmstrips, activity books, achievement tests, word cards, placement tests, and teacher's guides. Accordingly, we recommend the purchase of the reading-readiness books, the twenty-three workbooks, and the half-dozen activities books, the latter of which are, unlike most, challenging and fun. Some parents may find the teacher's guides helpful, at least at the outset.

Some children may not need sequentially or-

---

*The series was recently acquired from McGraw Hill by Phoenix Learning Resources, 468 Park Avenue South, New York, New York 10016.

dered supplementary reading and, like Grant, pick up
the basics in the Sullivan Readers and not be intimidated by more demanding—and sometimes con-
fusing—materials. For those who seem to require
more practice at each level, the McGraw-Hill Economy Reading Series and the accompanying activities
books are very good. But again, we would caution
against overloading the child with materials that are
more appropriate to the classroom than to learning.
Age-graded readers of the kind suggested here may
be helpful to one child but not to another, or may be
useful at one point in his or her development but not at
another. The Economy Reading Series consists of
some sixteen texts and as many activities books, but
the homeschooled child may need only a few or, as in
the case of two of our own children, none.*

A good rule-of-thumb is to proceed through any
given series one book at a time, and to be prepared to
abandon it and look for alternatives if for one reason or
another it doesn't work.

WRITING

Not penmanship, but rather the development
of the ability to communicate in writing concerns us
here. There are, of course, dozens of books on the

---

*The Economy Reading Series list can be obtained from McGraw-
Hill, Inc., School Division, Box 25308, Oklahoma City, OK 73125.

subject, and many of them are well done and quite useful. Unfortunately, most of them address those who have had at least *some* writing experience and need to sharpen their skills. Where does the child with no experience begin?

Again, it is simpler than those who talk about "expressive skills" and "language arts" would have us believe. It is merely a matter of providing the child with *examples*, *opportunities*, and *incentive* to write.

We began by having our children keep a daily journal—almost from the time they were able to pick up a pencil or crayon. When they were very young and at the scribbling stage we would encourage them to give titles to their drawings—"Mom," "A House," or whatever—and copy the words (which we would print out for them on a separate sheet) on to the page, which they would save. As they became more articulate, we would have them dictate to one of us what they wanted to record, which we would write down—at first in block letters, and later in script—and have them copy into the journal. Before too long, they would be writing entries on their own, and all we had to do was be available to help with the spelling of words or help formulate an idea or observation. Almost anything could find its way into those early notebooks: weather reports, what we were doing or planned to do that day or week, the comings and goings of friends and relatives, fragments of conversations, moods, and, to a lesser extent (since entries were not intended to be as personal and private as they might be in a diary, for example), hopes, fears, triumphs, and disappointments. The primary incentive to maintain the notebooks was that we took them seriously: they were treated as sources of information and daily accounts of our activities. "When did we plant the corn?" or "Didn't we get that last batch of Hubbards in mid-June?" Micki might ask one morning after breakfast, and the boys would be expected to locate the answer somewhere in their notebooks. Because the notebooks were useful to all of us, their writing was regularly reviewed and frequently the target of generally good-natured criticism. Reed's failure to record an important event might be noted by Drew, for instance, whose undue preoccupation with the weather might in turn draw Grant's attention. The experience of getting words—however few—down on paper on a regular basis, of having them taken seriously, and of learning to respond to criticism, made writing a *natural* and *useful* activity rather than a series of exercises in developing "language skills." And as the notebooks were maintained over the years, we were able to encourage the boys to regularly review their earlier work and compare it with what they were doing in the present so as to develop a sense of continuity and progress.

Another "real-world" activity that effectively fostered writing skills—both in form and in content— was letter and note writing. In an era when "reaching out and touching someone" is more likely to involve a telephone than pen and paper, the fine art of letter writing may very well be in decline, but children who are introduced to the practice at an early age will generally enjoy writing to Grandma to thank her for the birthday gift.

The process is similar to the one we used with the notebooks: one of us would carefully print out what the child wanted to say—and it was made clear that "Dear Grandma, thanks for the gift, Love Reed" just isn't adequate—which he would then copy on a folded sheet which he had illustrated. Later, we would do the same in script, and, again, before too long he would be doing it all on his own.

And as with the notebooks, the notes and letters were routinely subjected to review and comment: "That's not much of a letter to Aunt Grace," Micki might admonish one of the boys. "Do it again and this time tell her what we've been doing." Sometimes this would be resisted, of course, but in the process, the give-and-take, standards of performance, of content and form, evolved in a meaningful fashion.

From the above, it should be clear that we believe that learning to read and write should be a pleasant and uncomplicated experience, and needs not resemble the frustrating and painful process it so often becomes in a conventional school setting. A relatively small number of *meaningful* reading and writing exercises, combined with the kinds and range of activities suggested in earlier chapters, will almost certainly ensure the acquisition of these skills painlessly and with greater effectiveness than the schools are ordinarily able to provide.

But again, we need to stress *individual differences*. Not only will children learn at different ages, as we have already noted, but they will in all likelihood manifest different levels of interest in reading and, perhaps even more so, in writing. Grant had written *Boys and Girls of Mayan Days*, a collection of short stories, by the time he was ten, and followed this with his autobiography not too long afterwards before publishing a series of articles for dairy goat journals. Drew, in contrast, showed relatively little interest in doing much more than his daily journal (and, it is generally agreed, did the best job of any of them in this regard), until he began doing a weekly column on astronomy for the local newspaper. Much along the same lines, Reed showed almost no interest in writing until he took up the editorship of his regional running club monthly newsletter.

Perhaps the point has to be made here—and we shall reiterate it after dealing with the "third R"—is that in these early years when the basics are being laid down, it is more important to provide the child with a sense of accomplishment and to build self-esteem than to overload him or her with exercises that very well may provide "the basics"—but in the process make it all but impossible for him or her to put them to good use later on.

ARITHMETIC

It is the most intimidating of the three R's, and perhaps for good reason. Too many of us remember too many days and evenings doing page after page of math problems, and, too often, getting worse and worse at it as time went on. (Cartoonist Gary Larson's vision of Hell as an amusement arcade filled with "story problem machines" probably strikes a responsive chord in more than a few of us.) And not surprisingly, since one of the primary functions of grade school math, it is generally understood, is to sort and track, rather than impart analytic or reasoning skills.

But since homeschooled children do not need to be sorted or tracked, time can be spent providing the child with both computational and reasoning skills without overloading him or her with alienating busywork. The general objectives are clear enough: children need to be able to do addition, subtraction, multiplication, and division, with reasonable speed and accuracy. But one cannot justifiably attempt to dictate just *how* fast, *how* accurate, or *when* these skills should be in place. Curriculum organizers and

school administrators have the answers, of course—
their professional identity requires it—but, typically,
their rhetoric is at considerable variance with their
performance: children acquire the basics—if, indeed,
they do at all—at widely, sometimes wildly, varying
ages, and efforts to impart these skills by loading them
up with busywork cannot help but result in failures on
the order of those seen in our public schools today.

Our experience suggests that children should
be exposed to math very early and very gently, so that
over the early childhood years it comes to be regarded
as, if not exactly *fun*, at least interesting, unintimidat-
ing, and even challenging. The usual toddler items—
blocks, puzzles, and books—will go a long way in
stimulating interest in mathematical relationships and
concepts, and parents should probably generally refrain from imposing anything in the way of a formal
math program upon him or her until the child shows a
genuine interest in learning how to carry out operations. Ideally, at this point a math series comparable
to the *Sullivan Readers*, one that would make learning math as enjoyable as learning to read, would be
available. Unfortunately, no such program exists. The
programmed math books we have examined and used
on a short-term basis proved unsatisfactory, primarily
because they do not provide enough opportunities—
minimal as we think these need be—for *practice*. On
the other hand, most conventional elementary-level
math workbooks are too heavily weighted in the other

direction: there is too much in the way of largely meaningless problem solving—so much so, in fact, that it is more likely to turn off the ordinarily intelligent child than to inspire or sharpen skills. In short, teaching and learning the "third R" take a bit more experimentation and effort than do the other two.

After fairly extensive searching and some experimentation, we adopted the Laidlaw *Spectrum Mathematics* workbooks (2nd edition, 1980), not because they are especially well-done (in fact, too many of the examples provided complicate rather than clarifying some fairly basic operations) but because they present materials systematically and without the busywork characteristic of most other elementary math books. They put what we regarded as an undue emphasis on word problems—which we generally ignored.

The series consists of seven books, completion of which should provide the preteen with an adequate foundation in mathematics. One needs to be aware, however, that precisely because the series moves along in an orderly and no-nonsense manner, a child may occasionally require additional practice in an area before proceeding to the next topic. When we encountered such a situation, we simply prepared additional practice problems, and, in general, didn't hesitate to slow down, speed up, or skip sections in order to accommodate individual abilities and interests. Our main objective, it should be emphasized, was to maintain involvement while imparting basic skills. In recognition of the fact that math is not inherently interesting to many children, we chose to err on the side of demanding too little rather than too much in order to make the subject as agreeable as possible and without having to resort to gimmicks.

A BASICS POTPOURRI

Learning the basics needs not—should not—be as austere or as linear a process as might be implied by the above. A steady diet of the same old workbooks and exercises, however carefully monitored, becomes tedious. Fortunately, variety can be injected into the basics program by way of several sets of workbooks designed to supplement a more conventional academic regimen, but useful in the early phases of the kind of homeschooling program outlined above. These "supermarket workbooks," which are widely available in markets and discount stores, include the *Golden Step Ahead* math, reading, science, and social studies books from the publishers of the highly regarded Golden Books (Western Publishing Company), the *Honor Roll Achievement Books* of Harbor House, and the *School Zone* series by the publishing company of that name.

Each of these series consists of about 50 thirty-two-page workbooks which vary widely in quality and usefulness. At two dollars each they are, unfortunately, overpriced, but parents can very selectively utilize them as change-of-pace materials, for they are generally quite effective in capturing and holding children's interest and do occasionally touch upon topics that might be overlooked or ignored in more conventional workbooks. The *Golden Step Ahead* series is the flashiest and most consistent of the three, although some parents may reasonably object to its pop-culture tone, "reward stickers" mentality, and—common to all three series—the categorizing of materials by grade levels. Our practice was to use them very selectively.

KEEPING IT SIMPLE

But is this *enough*? We think it is, only because we believe that, in general, too much of what is imposed upon the child in schools in the name of teaching him or her basics is in fact a mechanism for sorting children into *organizationally manageable categories*—the "bright," "average," and "slow," or, more extremely, those deserving "enrichment" programs and those requiring "special education."

Homeschooling parents, of course, are under no such constraints, and can approach the task of providing their children with the basics in a nonbureaucratic, even leisurely fashion, and time ordinarily spent on "basics busywork" in the classroom can be devoted to intrinsically more interesting and rewarding educational activities, many of which do not require a mastery of the Three R's. There is plenty of time between infancy and adolescence to acquire basic reading, writing, and computational skills, and too much too soon, in an effort to conform to bureaucratic norms and fill the space of childhood, is almost certain to do more damage than a program that allows the child to set his or her own pace, follow his or her own lead, and, most importantly, keep the spark of interest alive through these early, terribly impressionable years.*

---

*Sir Karl Popper, in his autobiography, *Unended Quest*, remarks, "The three R's . . . are, I think, the only essentials a child has to be taught, and some children do not even need to be taught in order to learn these. *Everything else is atmosphere, and learning through reading and thinking.* [Emphasis ours.] (Open Court, 1982), p. 12.

CHAPTER 8

Beyond Basics

The basics, combined with a rich mix of special activities, projects, and general reading, should provide almost any child with more than enough in the way of opportunities well into the teen-age years. And once basic reading, writing, and computational skills are in place—generally, around the age of ten or twelve—the child is ready for new challenges.

Precisely what forms these should take will, ideally, vary from child to child in accord with his or her interests and abilities. If the groundwork has been laid, at this point the child will have acquired basic skills and will be able to handle increasingly complex and more demanding materials with relative ease. Some children will move quickly into pre-algebra and science, while others may develop interests in litera-

ture or the fine arts. Here, and to perhaps a greater
extent than earlier, it is the child's and parents' joint
responsibility to locate materials that will serve these
interests and facilitate growth. This is, admittedly, no
easy task: at this juncture parental involvement in
education typically declines precipitously, and the
quality and content of middle- and high-school courses
are left to the authorities. One result of this distancing
of parents from the educational process is that it
becomes difficult to *locate*, much less *evaluate* higher-
level texts. Mere adoption of a text by a school system
is no guarantee of quality: the widely lamented but
largely unchecked watering-down and sanitizing of
texts in order to make them acceptable to various
constituencies and pressure groups make it increasingly difficult to find texts of value in virtually every
area. Over the years we have, through a process of
trial and error, identified some which we can recommend without reservations, others which do the job
but are less than inspiring, and a few which are simply
the best of a bad lot. There are others, of course, that
we may not know about, or which have recently come
on the market, which parents and children may want
to review. What follows is what we regard as "state of
the art" but is by no means an authoritative list.
Indeed, in the areas of science, government, and
history, we hope that better books are out there or
being written, given the general mediocrity of those
we were able to locate.

ENGLISH GRAMMAR

It is perhaps the most basic of the basics, but one that probably doesn't need to be *systematically* examined until the middle-school years. The parent who has routinely corrected the child's written and spoken English over the years will have provided a sense of proper usage; an understanding of the rational—or occasionally irrational—basis for such usage requires more. This is provided in perhaps the very best of texts, the six-volume *English Grammar and Composition* series by John E. Warriner et al. (Harcourt Brace Jovanovich, 1977). Comprehensive—they total nearly three thousand pages—the series begins with a "First Course" that can be used by most younger teen-agers without assistance, and concludes with a "Complete Course" that will provide the college-bound senior with an overview of all that went before. Unlike too many books that purport to make grammar and composition "interesting," the Warriner series is rigorous, comprehensive, and authoritative, and as such needs to be taken in small doses. Our experience has been that intermittent and selective— we generally ignored the composition exercises—use of this series over a half-dozen years provides the child with superior language skills.

ENGLISH COMPOSITION

As we indicated in the previous chapter, most of the more worthwhile books on writing are addressed to those who have had some experience at it. And by the age of ten or twelve, the child who has kept a journal and written letters, can benefit from exposure to the best of these. One of our standards here was that they provide the young writer with a useful way of looking at what he or she is actually writing rather than with a series of exercises (which we discouraged on the grounds that their artificiality makes the writing process difficult, if not impossible, for the child to take seriously).

Foremost among these is the William Strunk and E. B. White little classic, *The Elements of Style* (Macmillan, many editions), a paperback of some seventy-five pages that is more useful than most composition texts many times its size. It is a book for younger as well as older children; we urged our children to read, reread, and read it yet again as they grew older.

A close second is William Zinsser's *On Writing Well* (Harper and Row, 2nd revised edition, 1980), which is especially useful in showing the young writer how to edit his or her writing, and in explaining why this is important. This, like Strunk and White, is a book to be read and reread over these formative years.

In a different category—and to be generally avoided—are books with titles such as *Modern Rhetoric, Patterns of Exposition,* and *The High School Essay,* most of which in their didactic intensity turn what should be an opportunity to develop narrative and expressive skills into drudgery. Indeed, one of the genuine accomplishments of high school English as currently taught is the inculcation of a general aversion to writing.

If writing is not turned into an ordeal, very few children will find it difficult to write, although learning to write *well* will ordinarily take some time and practice. But what about the teen-ager who cannot seem to get *anything,* good or bad, down on paper? Natalie Goldberg's *Writing Down the Bones* (Shambala, 1986), with its reassuring "trust yourself" approach, may prove useful in breaking a juvenile writer's block. If not, time and the development of interests and experiences that are felt to be worth writing about, may be all that are necessary. In the half dozen years between childhood and adulthood there is more than enough time to acquire this skill— as well as others. Patience, informed by a recognition of individual differences, will prove more effective than the best of texts insensitively imposed.

MATHEMATICS

Parents and children who have used the Spectrum Mathematics series that was recommended with reservations in the last chapter will find that the Laidlaw higher-math series is a distinct improvement. The first volume, *Preparing to Use Algebra*, by Albert Shuite and Robert Peterson (4th edition, 1986), which can be effectively introduced when the child is about midway through the last of the Spectrum books, will require a greater degree of parental involvement than those that follow, mainly to familiarize the student with the format. *Using Algebra* (by Kenneth Travers, et al., 2nd edition, 1984) and *Using Geometry* (by David Wells, et al., 1984) require little more than the availability of the teacher's edition to check answers to problems. *Using Advanced Algebra* (by Kenneth Travers, et al., 2nd edition, 1984), the last in this series, will prepare the student for Raymond A. Barnett's *Functions and Graphs: A Precalculus Course* (McGraw-Hill, 1985), supplemented with the *Instructor's Manual* (by Fred Safier, McGraw-Hill, 1985).

BASIC SCIENCE

Three excellent elementary science texts are available in the McGraw-Hill "Challenges to Science" series: *Life Science* (by William L. Smallwood, 1978), *Earth Science* (by Robert Heller, et al., 1979), and *Physical Science* (by George Williams, et al., 1979). Each of these is conceptually sound and well-written. Science-oriented students will be able to handle these earlier, but they are intended for middle-school-level students and can be mastered by them with little or no help from parents or more advanced siblings— although they should be prepared to be recruited to help with the simple laboratory activities presented in each chapter.

Of the three sciences typically studied at the high-school level, biology is perhaps the best served by texts. *Biology*, by William L. Smallwood and Peter Alexander (Silver Burdett, 1981), ranked first among the many biology texts we examined, primarily because it presented, in a very traditional and uncluttered way, the basic terms and concepts of biology. Very different in its approach and considerably more difficult is the Biological Sciences Curriculum Study group's *Biological Science: A Molecular Approach* (D. C. Heath, 4th edition, 1980), which, with the

Teacher's Guide provides a more contemporary and dynamic account of what is happening in the field.

Because of their special interests in this area, Grant and Drew went on to use, respectively, A. M. Winchester, *Genetics* (Houghton Mifflin, 1977) and William A. Jensen and Frank B. Salisbury, *Botany: An Ecological Approach* (Wadsworth, 1972), both college-level texts.

After several false starts, we settled for Paul G. Hewitt, *Conceptual Physics* (Little, Brown, 4th edition, 1981), which was less comprehensive than we would have liked but more accessible than anything else we could locate. And perhaps the least satisfactory of the science texts, owing largely, we suspect, to the nature of the subject, was William L. Masterson and Emil J. Slowinski, *Chemical Principles* (Saunders, 4th edition, 1977).

These two subjects, along with the foreign languages, required by far the greatest amount of outside support of any element in our homeschooling program. Here, when necessary, the boys called upon the expertise of friends, relatives, and the staff at the local colleges, and were able to cover these topics satisfactorily, if not with the same sense of mastery as in other areas.

HISTORY AND GOVERNMENT

These inherently interesting subjects were, we discovered, the worst served by textbooks. A review of literally dozens of texts turned up a few that are useful in providing an overview of government and history, but none which merited the kind of systematic attention the science texts received.

In fact, it was not until well after the boys had been exposed to a wide variety of historical literature and documents that we recommended anything in the way of texts, and we did so with the understanding that this was only to ensure that there were no major gaps in their knowledge.

This was a comfortable arrangement that acknowledged that one probably acquires a better understanding of American history by reading Dos Passos' *U.S.A.* or Steinbeck's *The Grapes of Wrath* than from a textbook account of the period, and that a thoughtful reading of The Declaration of Independence and the Constitution of the United States is preferable to studying what a textbook author *says* these documents are about.

But after the student has had an opportunity to read widely, if desultorily—about the Maya and the Egyptians, the kings and queens of England and

France, the civil rights movement, the exploration of
Africa, church history, and biographies of great and
not-so-great men and women, it may be useful for
them to spend at least a few weeks—not all together—
reviewing a text or two that attempt to put events
into perspective. For this purpose, we recommend the
unfortunately out-of-print and somewhat dated, *The
American Pageant: A History of the Republic* (D. C.
Heath, 1956), by Thomas Bailey, which is especially
lucid, and Gerald Leinwand's *The Pageant of World
History* (Allyn and Bacon, 1977), which is rather
superficial, but provides something of a synoptic
perspective on events.

LITERATURE

A high-school English teacher with many years'
experience once told us that she had never known a
student to read a book by an author he or she had first
encountered in a literature textbook. An overstate-
ment, perhaps, but the point is well taken: literature
textbooks too often seem intended to inoculate against
interest in literature rather than inspire it. For those
who are unlikely to read widely or well upon completion of their formal education, these texts may serve
the purpose of providing them with perhaps the only
encounters they will ever have with "great writers"—
on the dubious assumption that this is in some way a

worthwhile thing to experience. A bit of Poe, a dab of Melville, a smattering of Shakespeare, and perhaps a dollop of Thurber or even Updike, and one is prepared for the world of Gothic novels, sitcoms, and soap operas.

But the child who has developed a love of reading has little need of such exposure. Here, again, texts are marginally useful, primarily as sources of information about what *others* are reading and why. When they were in their mid-teens we had the boys scan two series—the D. C. Heath "Living Literature Series" (6 volumes, 1981), and the "Ginn Literature Series" (6 volumes, 1986)—to identify authors whose works they might be interested in reading; each declared it a waste of time. By then their reading extended far beyond the confines of the high-school anthologies.

FOREIGN LANGUAGES

As almost anybody who has attempted to do so will acknowledge, languages are difficult to learn in isolation. One can memorize mathematical and chemical formulas, diagram sentences, and decipher hieroglyphics in private, but few can master a foreign language without speaking it and hearing it spoken.

Accordingly, this posed something of a problem for our homeschooling program. We once knew Latin,

French, and Russian, but were entirely unprepared to
converse in any of these; moreover, Grant, with his
interest in Latin America, was anxious to learn
Spanish. We discovered that the University of California offered several correspondence courses in Spanish,
and Grant enrolled. The results were, predictably
enough, mixed: he learned to read and write Spanish,
but learned to speak it only later, in college courses in
which he discovered that it came very easily.

Drew and Reed approached it differently. We
purchased a set of highly recommended Foreign
Language Institute tapes and manuals which Drew
worked through over a two-year period and found far
from satisfactory. Reed, benefiting from his brothers'
experiences, joined the local Spanish soccer team,
developed an ear for the language, and has had the
easiest time of the three. If there is a lesson here, it
would seem to be that there is no easy homeschooling
road to learning a foreign language.

What about physical education, music, art,
geography, health, and all of the other requirements
that clutter the conventional curriculum? They are
very important, of course, but homeschoolers will
define these in different ways. It is up to them to
decide what form "physical education" will take, for
example, and whether it is better to learn to play the
piano or to learn art history. Our task in this chapter
has been primarily to identify the best *core* mate-

rials—texts around which individualized reading lists and special projects *may* be organized—and most emphatically not to present a homeschooling *curriculum* as such. Our intent, in short, has been to encourage flexibility rather than issue directives as to how an upper-level homeschooling program might be put together.

CHAPTER 9

Beyond Homeschooling

Our goal in homeschooling has always been to educate our children—to facilitate the development of intellect and character—and not merely to prepare them for college or a career. Of course we assumed that they would go to college just as we had, and we were not especially concerned about their gaining entry to a reasonably good school because we knew that they were being better prepared than most conventionally educated college-bound students.

It was not until Grant was fifteen that we began to check out options and requirements. First there was the question of costs. We had been homesteading for nearly a decade and putting any surplus we had been able to extract back into the ranch, and were apprehensive about how we would be able to finance this, the first of what were likely to be several college educations. The so-called inexpensive colleges were hardly that; a year at a state college then cost approximately $4,000, and the University of California schools (the state has a two-tier system) cost half again as much. Of course there were the community colleges, but the nearest one had, if anything, a worse reputation than the local school district. Costs at private colleges were as much as twice as high as at public institutions, but this was of no real concern to us as there were few on the West Coast—where the tradition of private higher education is not as strong as in the East—that we found attractive.

As we reviewed the possibilities we found that many of the elite schools—those in the Ivy League and another dozen or so public and private institutions— might in fact be less expensive than some less renowned schools because their large endowments enabled them to underwrite more comprehensive scholarship and financial aid packages—for those who gained admittance. But the competition for admission was formidable: only one out of every ten to fifteen applicants was successful.

Here our homeschooling effort came up against its first real test. *We* were happy with our program, but how would it *test out*? Grant wrote well, read widely, and could hold his own in virtually any social situation. How would these translate into the kinds of things college admissions officers look for when reviewing applications?

The first hurdle was the Scholastic Aptitude Test—the "SAT." We had heard of it, of course, but until this point had paid it no attention. Now we who had eschewed testing were confronted with it. Grant dutifully registered, took the practice tests, and one Saturday morning entered a high-school classroom to be academically tested for the first time in his life. A few months later he took three more tests—the "Achievement Tests" generally required for consideration for admission to many colleges—in English, mathematics, and biology. His scores were in the ninetieth to ninety-ninth percentiles.

Later that year Grant interviewed at nearly a dozen colleges and applied to two. We submitted a letter to each, describing his course work and evaluating his strengths and weaknesses as objectively as possible. In lieu of teacher and counselor recommendations, Grant provided letters from a half dozen people who could variously attest to his work in the community health center, his dairy goat business, and, in general, his character and intellectual potential. He wrote a long essay that described his years on the ranch, his homeschooling experiences, and his hopes for the future. He was admitted to Yale and Harvard and entered the latter that fall.

Two years later Drew followed a similar course

and joined Grant at Harvard, where both majored in biology. Reed entered Harvard in the fall of 1988.

As the late John Holt correctly observed when Grant's admission to Harvard was receiving widespread publicity, a homeschooling program should not be considered a success or failure on the basis of whether or not a child is admitted to an elite college. Homeschooling programs have, and should have, different objectives, derived from the interests and needs of the children and parents. Our program reflected, in what one homeschooler called its "practical bookishness," our academic and ranch experiences, and well served our boys when it came time to apply to colleges. Had we been homeschoolers who had been, say, boat builders, musicians, or artists, it would have been different in at least some respects—and almost certainly less conventionally college-preparatory. Perhaps Grant would have by now become a master boat builder, Drew a sophomore at Juilliard, and Reed a sculptor.

But to the extent that college attendance is regarded as evidence of the effectiveness of secondary school preparation—and conventional schools, for better or worse, are commonly rated by such criteria—homeschoolers have little to be concerned about. A homeschooled student who does reasonably well on a few standardized tests and can make a case for himself or herself, will have little difficulty attracting the attention of admission directors of most good colleges.

As one remarked after reading Grant's submission, "We get very weary of reading application after application from students who are first in their class and captain of the football team. It's refreshing to come across someone who is *different.*" Of course there will be the occasional bureaucrat who will find it all incomprehensible, such as the Johns Hopkins interviewer who told Grant that he would have to apply as a *foreign student,* or the junior college dean who informed a homeschooling parent that he would not, on principle, admit any student who did not have a *diploma.* Homeschoolers who encounter such mindlessness would do well to seek other academic options, for they are, as we discovered, more plentiful and accommodating than is commonly assumed.

CHAPTER 10

Some Homeschooling
Questions and Answers

Still, there will be questions: Is homeschooling the best thing for *my* child? How can I be sure? What if he isn't interested in reading? Can I get in trouble with the law? Is there a homeschooling program I can use? What about socialization?

Over the years hundreds of homeschoolers and would-be homeschoolers have called and written to us with questions like these. Some are trivial, while others raise important issues. Here, in no particular order, are those we have heard most frequently.

Q. *What about the law?*
A. Homeschooling is legal in most states. In

some the filing of an affidavit is necessary, while others
require nothing at all. In a few states—such as North
Dakota, for example—homeschooling can become extremely difficult. Appendix 5 provides a state-by-state
legal summary, but it should be noted that occasionally—and sometimes in blatant disregard of the law—a
publicity-seeking district attorney or a vindictive
school administrator will make life difficult for a
homeschooling family by charging violations of school
attendance laws. Fortunately, these assaults have
been generally unsuccessful, but they have often been
costly in terms of the time and money spent defending
homeschooling.

Q. *What about the socialization of homeschooled children? Aren't they too isolated from their
peers?*

A. In the first place, homeschooled children are
seldom, if ever, socially isolated. Indeed, precisely
because they have more opportunities to interact with
a wide range of people, they tend to become socially
competent and socially responsible at an earlier age
than most of their conventionally schooled peers. The
argument that socialization is the *primary* function of
the schools—and educators are increasingly claiming
just that as their failure to develop the intellect
becomes more and more obvious—ignores evidence
that peer group pressure in the schools, except in
some very special contexts, does little to foster

intellectual growth or the acquisition of desirable social values.

Q. My child is in junior high school and not doing very well. Should I consider homeschooling?

A. Yes, but it should be something you discuss from the outset with your child. We think it is important that parents and students in such situations approach the idea of homeschooling very tentatively and recognize that they need not make a long-term commitment. Sometimes a semester or two away from school is all that is necessary to get things into perspective.

Q. You both have had experience as teachers. How important is that?

A. We don't think it is very important at all, except insofar as it made us aware of the shortcomings of the schools. Almost any reasonably intelligent parent who has made it through the pre-school years without too much trouble has the ability and experience to do a good job of homeschooling as long as it continues to be regarded, by parents and children alike, as something of an adventure and not an ordeal.

Q. But how do you prevent burnout? I've been homeschooling my children for several years and I'm worn out.

A. You've probably been taking yourself too

seriously. Back off and give yourself *and* the children some space—physical, emotional, and intellectual. Take a break for a few weeks—or even a few months—and see what happens. You will probably discover that the children do quite well on their own.

Q. *Why don't you recommend any of the prepackaged curriculums that have been developed for the homeschooling market?*

A. Primarily because most of them merely mimic public school curriculums and are rigid, age-graded, and test-oriented. Others are just not very good even by conventional standards. We have not seen very much that has been specifically designed for homeschoolers that hasn't been done better or less expensively for the general market. Finally, we object to the *dependency* on prepackaged materials that these foster. To be truly effective, homeschooling needs to encourage independence and critical thinking and this is lost when one set of authorities—public school administrators—is exchanged for another—homeschooling "experts" and their products.

Q. *I've been homeschooling for years, but suddenly all my teen-aged son wants to do is read hot-rod magazines. Now what?*

A. You should respect—and exploit—this interest. Encourage him to talk, read, and write about it, and provide him with resources that will allow him to develop this interest in such a way as to make the best use of his special abilities and talents. Schools ordinarily cannot tolerate—much less encourage—eccentric interests, but homeschooling parents can—and should. (See Appendix 7.)

Q. How do you deal with relatives? My in-laws disapprove of homeschooling.

A. Unless they are paying off your mortgage, ignore them. If they persist, suggest that they foot the bill for a second-rate but entirely respectable education at an expensive private school. Or send them a copy of this book.

Q. You've homeschooled your children on a ranch. Wouldn't it have been impossible in the city?

A. It certainly would have been different, but by no means impossible. If fact, some of the most successful homeschoolers we know live in the very heart of the city, and tell us that they would find it very hard to homeschool their children in the country!

Q. For two-parent families—and especially those in which the mother stays at home and takes care of the children—homeschooling might be possible. But what about single-parent families, or those in which both parents are employed outside the home?

A. Of course some circumstances make it harder than others. Sometimes tradeoffs can be made, with a parent giving up outside employment—and the extra family income—to take on primary responsibility for homeschooling, for example. Many families will not be able to afford this, however, and single parents, especially, will find it difficult to homeschool. Some have been able to do so by rescheduling their work hours, others by arranging to work at home, and yet others by enlisting the help of sympathetic relatives and neighbors. It would be misleading to suggest that any parent, regardless of circumstances, should be able to work it out, but in many instances it comes down to a matter of priorities and how these are ordered.

Q. What if your child runs into trouble with math or science and you can't help?

A. That's easy. There is always help available out there in friends, neighbors, older brothers and sisters, and other relatives, and children who have learned how to learn, how to ask questions, will find that there is always somebody ready to provide assistance when their parents can't help.

Q. Still, shouldn't children learn to take tests? How else can they or their parents know how they are doing?

A. Parents and children continually engage in an evaluation process in the give-and-take of homeschooling so they generally have a pretty good idea of just how well things are going. It is the assumption that parents need to know how well their children are doing *relative to others* that we find objectionable. Children who are given to understand that standardized tests are not necessarily valid measures of worth or competence will not be much intimidated by them when they come up against them—and they will—but this kind of understanding comes with maturity. Children whose sense of themselves is derived, if only in part, from tests are as likely to be hurt as helped by them.

CHAPTER 11

Teaching Our Own— And Others

S ummer, 1987. Reed is in the computer room with six boys and girls ranging in ages from nine to sixteen. Drew, home from his first year at Harvard, is out on the ridge in the boys' cabin with four teen-agers who are doing biology and mathematics. We are in the living room with our English Composition "writers' workshop." We are nearing the end of the second of two four-week sessions of our first summer camp, our "tutorial on a working ranch."

Very much a family affair, it has been more successful than we had ever hoped. The sixteen-hour days jammed with chores, two-hour tutorials, construction, drama, hikes, ceramics, and sports, have been intense, but immensely rewarding. The fifteen boys and girls are learning many of the same things in much the same way as our boys did—through hands-on experience, in concentrated doses, in a setting in which they and their efforts are being taken seriously.

The idea originated in a discussion when Drew was home for Christmas vacation: Why not organize a camp in which we implemented some of our educational ideas? We roughed out a program in which we would do creative writing, Drew would be responsible for the sciences, Reed computers, and Garth general maintenance. Grant, unfortunately for us, was committed to spending the summer on a research project in Cambridge.

In the months that followed, we cleared land, erected a half-dozen structures—cabins, a field kitchen, study and dining area, and bathhouse—and prepared a brochure. By June, when Drew rejoined us, we were ready to go.

Over the next eight weeks we had ample opportunity to "field-test" some of our most cherished notions about how children can and should be educated. These two dozen campers, with their different backgrounds, were not, after all, *our* children, and we did not promise or expect to see major transformations take place in the four weeks we'd be working with any one of them. Nevertheless—and this is the reason for this epilogue—we found that the methods

and assumptions that we had employed in teaching our
own children over the years were entirely applicable
and surprisingly effective in these circumstances. We
found that most of these children—including those
well into their teens and and those who attended good
public schools—had had very little in the way of direct
feedback and review of their work, and were, almost
without exception, enthusiastic participants. That
they were responsible for setting and monitoring their
pace and progress was a novel concept, but it did not
take long for them to realize that learning could be a
rewarding experience—and even fun. In a sense, their
response validated our approach to learning, for it
showed that most children—and not only our own—
want to learn and will do so readily if given a chance.
It is a lesson that we—parents and educators alike—
need to take to heart if we are serious about encouraging excellence in education.

Appendices

APPENDIX 1

A Homeschooling
Reference Library

This list is illustrative, rather than "authoritative," the result of some fifteen years of accumulating books to meet our homeschooling reference needs. Some of these we consult almost daily, others seasonally, and still others very rarely, but each has proven valuable in its own time and way. Those we find most generally useful are marked with an asterisk.

Atlas of the Solar System. Patrick Moore and Gary Hunt. Rand McNally, 1983. One of Drew's valued resources.

The Book of Lists. Irving Wallace, et al. Bantam, various dates and volumes. Sometimes trivial and even silly, but always engaging.

Burnham's Celestial Handbook. Robert Burnham, Jr. 3 volumes, Dover, 1983.

The Concise Oxford Dictionary of English Literature. Dorothy Eagle. Oxford, 1985. One of the series of Oxford paperback references too inexpensive not to have on the shelf.

The Concise Oxford Dictionary of Quotations. Oxford, 1985. Nearly 6,000 quotations by over a thousand writers, for less than ten dollars.*

Contemporary Poets. James Vinson, ed. St. James/St. Martin's. 1975.

A Dictionary of Catch Phrases. Eric Partridge. Stein and Day, 1977.

Dictionary of Foreign Terms. M. Pei and S. Ramondino. Dell, 1974.

The Dictionary of Misinformation. Tom Burnam. Harper, 1986. "The book to set the record straight."

Dictionary of Problem Words and Expressions. Henry Shaw. McGraw-Hill, 1975.

A Dictionary of Slang and Unconventional English. 7th edition. Eric Partridge. Macmillan, 1970.

The Elements of Style. 3rd edition. William Strunk, Jr., and E. B. White. Macmillam, 1979. For reading and reference.*

The Encyclopedia of American Facts and Dates. 8th edition. Gordon Carruth. Harper and Row, 1986. A compendium of information on American wars, government, arts, and entertainment.*

Familiar Quotations. John Bartlett. Little, Brown, 1955. A conventional education, of sorts, in itself.*

A Field Guide to the Birds. Roger Tory Peterson. Houghton Mifflin, 1947. A classic.*

The Filmgoer's Companion. 6th edition. Leslie Halliwell. Avon, 1976. For our movie buffs. Quirky, but relatively comprehensive.

Find it Fast. Robert I. Berkman. Harper and Row, 1987. "How to uncover expert information on any subject."

Flowers of the World. Frances Perry. Bonanza Books, 1972.

Golden Field Guides: Birds; Seashells; Trees; National Parks. Various dates and editors. Golden Press.*

Golden Nature Guides. Some fifty different titles ranging from *Birds* to *Zoology.* Inexpensive, informative, colorful. Ideal for younger children. Golden Press, various dates and editions.*

Guinness Sports Record Book. Norris McWhirter. Bantam, 1980.

Guinness Book of World Records. Norris McWhirter. Sterling, 1986.*

The Harmony Illustrated Encyclopedia of Jazz. 3rd edition. Brian Case and Stan Britt. Salamander Books, 1986.

How Did They Do That? Caroline Sutton. Quill, 1984. "Wonders of the far and recent past explained."

How Do They Do That? Caroline Sutton. Quill, 1984. "Wonders of the modern world explained."

How Does It Work? Richard M. Koff. Signet, 1961. The kind of useful paperback likely to show up on used bookstore shelves.

The Illustrated Encyclopedia of the Animal Kingdom. 20 volumes. Danbury Press, 1971.

The Illustrated Encyclopedia of Black Music. Mike Clifford. Harmony Books, 1982.

Information U.S.A. Michael Lesko, Viking, 1986. More than you'll ever need to know about the federal government.

The Little, Brown Book of Anecdotes. Clifton Fadiman, ed. Little, Brown, 1985.

The Modern Researcher. Jacques Barzun and Henry F. Graff. Harcourt, Brace, 1962. Readable and indispensable.*

The Movie Quote Book. Harry Haun. Harper and Row, 1983.

The New Guide to Modern World Literature. Martin Seymour-Smith. Peter Bedrick Books, 1985. Opinionated, cranky, and comprehensive.*

The New York Times Guide to Reference Materials. Mona McCormick. Popular Library, 1971. A concise paperback.*

Oxford American Dictionary. Avon, 1980. One of several that we've worn out over the years. The *Oxford* is a sturdy, useful paperback.*

The Oxford Classical Dictionary. 2nd edition. N. G. L. Hammond and H. H. Scullard. Oxford, 1977.

The Oxford Dictionary of English Etymology. C. T. Onion, ed. Oxford, 1976.

The Oxford Guide to the English Language. E. S. C. Weiner and J. M. Hawkins. Oxford, 1984.

The Penguin Dictionary of Modern Quotations. J. M. and M. J. Cohen. Penguin, 1985.*

The People's Almanac. David Wallechinsky and Irving Wallace. Doubleday, 1975. "A reference book to be read with pleasure."*

Rand McNally Contemporary World Atlas. Rand McNally, 1985.*

Reader's Digest Complete Book of the Garden. Reader's Digest, 1966.

The Synonym Finder. J. I. Rodale. Warner, 1978. More useful than a thesaurus.*

The Times Atlas of World History. Geoffrey Barraclough, ed. Hammond, 1978. The ultimate historical atlas.*

The Viking Book of Aphorisms. W. H. Auden and Louis Kronenberger. Penguin, 1983.

The World Almanac and Book of Facts, 1987. Pharos Books, 1987.*

World Book. 22 volumes with annual supplements. Field Enterprises.*

APPENDIX 2

Children's Magazines:

Four Favorites

Cricket. A monthly selection of some of the best of children's stories, how-to articles, cartoons, and puzzles. Colorful and sprightly, eschews cuteness. Monthly. Box 2672, Boulder, CO 80231. $15.00.

Highlights for Children. A long-time favorite. Activities, stories, resources. Occasionally too aggressively didactic, but worthwhile if not taken too seriously. Monthly. 2300 W. Fifth Ave., Box 269, Columbus, OH 43216. $19.69.

National Geographic. Great photographs year after year. The one periodical almost everybody saves. Monthly. Box 2895, Washington, DC 20013. $18.00.

Natural History. Published by the American Museum of Natural History, this is for all ages. Probably the best nature writing and photography around. Monthly. Box 5000, Harlan, IA 51537. $20.00.

APPENDIX 3

Microscope Books for

Younger Readers

Beeler, Nelson F., and Franklyn M. Branley. *Experiments with a Microscope.* Crowell, 1957.

Headstrom, Richard, *Adventures with a Microscope.* Dover, 1977.

Johnson, Gaylord, and Maurice Bleifeld, *Hunting with a Microscope.* Arco, 1974.

Krauter, Dieter, *Experimenting with the Microscope.* Dover, 1968.

Ludovici, L. J., *The World of the Microscope*. Putnam, no date.

Simon, Seymour, *Exploring with a Microscope*. Random House, 1969.

APPENDIX 4

One Hundred (More or Less) Favorite Books Remembered

One of the most impor-
tant jobs any parent—
homeschooling or not—
has is that of encouraging the child's interest in
reading. Our children, as we have noted above, have
read hundreds of books, good, bad, and indifferent,
and have learned, we hope, to distinguish among
them. But what did they like? We asked them to try to
recall their twenty or so favorites, and the result, as
we might have expected, is something rather different
from the conventional "great books" list. There are a
few books here that we might not have chosen, and
others that we feel should have been included, but this
is their list and not ours. Some of their favorites

125

are children's classics, some are adult classics, and some are neither—and we leave it to the reader to decide which are which. Here then, in alphabetical order and in currently available editions, are their favorites.

The Adventures of Huckleberry Finn. Mark Twain. Bantam, 1988. (Drew, Reed).

The Adventures of Tom Sawyer. Mark Twain. Signet, 1980. (Drew).

The Age of Innocence. Edith Wharton. Scribner, 1983. (Grant).

All Quiet on the Western Front. Erich M. Remarque. Fawcett, 1987. (Grant).

The Architecture of the Arkansas Ozarks. Donald Harington. Harcourt, Brace, 1987. (Grant).

Banner in the Sky. James R. Ulman. Archway, 1984. (Garth).

A Bell for Adano. John Hersey. Knopf, 1944. (Reed).

The Caboose Who Got Loose. Bill Peet. Houghton Mifflin, 1971. (Drew).

The Call of the Wild. Jack London. Penguin, 1983. (Reed).

The Cat in the Hat. Dr. Seuss. Beginner, 1957. (Drew).

Catch Twenty-Two. Joseph Heller. Dell, 1985. (Drew).

Charlie and the Chocolate Factory. Roald Dahl. Bantam, 1986. (Garth, Drew).

Charlie and the Great Glass Elevator. Roald Dahl. Bantam, 1977. (Garth).

Charlotte's Web. E. B. White. Harper, 1952. (Garth).

The Chronicles of Narnia. C. S. Lewis. Collier Books, 1970. 7 vols. (Drew).

The Color Purple. Alice Walker. Washington Square Press, 1983. (Reed).

Crime and Punishment. Fyodor Dostoevsky. Penguin, 1952. (Reed).

Danny: The Champion of the World. Roald Dahl. Knopf, 1975. (Garth).

David Copperfield. Charles Dickens. Penguin, 1966. (Grant).

The Double Helix. James D. Watson. NAL, 1969. (Grant).

East of Eden. John Steinbeck. Penguin, 1979. (Grant, Drew).

Everything That Rises Must Converge. Flannery O'Connor. Farrar, Straus, and Giroux, 1965. (Reed).

The 500 Hats of Bartholomew Cubbins. Dr. Seuss. Vanguard, 1938. (Drew).

For Whom the Bell Tolls. Ernest Hemingway. Scribner, 1982. (Grant).

The Grapes of Wrath. John Steinbeck. Penguin, 1986. (Drew).

Green Eggs and Ham. Dr. Seuss. Beginner, 1960. (Grant, Drew).

Gulliver's Travels. Jonathan Swift. Penguin, 1967. (Reed).

Horton Hatches an Egg. Dr. Seuss. Random House, 1940. (Drew).

The Iliad. Homer. NAL, 1954. (Grant).

The Indian in the Cupboard. Lynne Reid Banks. Avon, 1982. (Garth).

James and the Giant Peach. Roald Dahl. Bantam, 1981. (Drew, Garth).

Johnny Got His Gun. Dalton Trumbo. Bantam, 1970. (Grant, Reed).

Johnny Tremain. Esther Forbes. Dell, 1987. (Garth).

Julie of the Wolves. Jean C. George. Harper, 1972. (Garth, Drew).

Kiss, Kiss. Roald Dahl. Knopf, 1959. (Drew, Reed).

Les Miserables. Victor Hugo. Fawcett, 1961. (Grant).

Light in August. William Faulkner. Random House, 1972. (Grant).

Little House in the Big Woods. Laura Ingalls Wilder. Harper and Row, 1971. (Garth).

Little House on the Prairie. Laura Ingalls Wilder. Harper and Row, 1971. (Garth).

McElligot's Pool. Dr. Seuss. Random House, 1947. (Drew).

The Monkey Wrench Gang. Edward Abbey. Avon, 1983. (Drew, Reed).

Mr. Popper's Penguins. Richard and Florence Atwater. Dell, 1986. (Garth).

Native Son. Richard Wright. Harper, 1986. (Drew, Reed).

Nineteen Eighty-Four. George Orwell. NAL, 1983. (Grant).

Of Mice and Men. John Steinbeck. Bantam, 1970. (Reed).

The Old Man and the Sea. Ernest Hemingway. Scribner, 1984. (Drew, Reed).

One Hundred Years of Solitude. Gabriel Garcia Marquez. Avon, 1971. (Grant).

The Pearl. John Steinbeck. Bantam, 1987. (Reed, Garth).

The Persian Boy. Mary Renault. Pantheon, 1972. (Grant).

The Portrait of Dorian Gray. Oscar Wilde. Dell, 1956. (Grant).

The Red Badge of Courage. Stephen Crane. Penguin, 1983. (Reed).

The Return of the Indian. Lynne Reid Banks. Avon, 1986. (Garth).

Sing Down the Moon. Scott O'Dell. Dell, 1976. (Garth).

Six Plays by Lillian Hellman. Random House, 1976. (Grant).

Stuart Little. E. B. White. Harper, 1945. (Garth, Reed, Drew).

Studs Lonigan. James T. Farrell. Avon, 1976. (Grant, Drew).

Tar Baby. Toni Morrison. NAL, 1983. (Grant).

Their Eyes Were Watching God. Zora Hurston. University of Illinois Press, 1978. (Grant).

Them. Joyce Carol Oates. Fawcett, 1986. (Grant).

Trumpet of the Swan. E. B. White. Harper, 1973. (Garth, Drew).

Twenty Thousand Leagues Under the Sea. Jules Verne. NAL, 1969. (Reed).

U.S.A. John Dos Passos. Houghton Mifflin, 1963. (Reed, Drew).

Watership Down. Richard Adams. Avon, 1975. (Drew, Garth).

Where the Wild Things Are. Maurice Sendak. Harper, 1984. (Drew).

Wise Blood. Flannery O'Connor. Farrar, Straus, and Giroux, 1965. (Grant).

World Book. Field Enterprises. Annual. 22 vols. (Drew).

The Wump World. Bill Peet. Houghton Mifflin, 1970. (Reed).

Yertle the Turtle and Other Stories. Dr. Seuss. Random House, 1958. (Drew).

APPENDIX 5

Homeschooling and the Law

State laws, as they pertain to homeschooling, are subject to various interpretations by state and local school officials and the courts. While the following should not be construed as legal advice, it is an attempt to briefly characterize state laws as of May 1, 1988. A number of these statutes are currently being challenged in the courts. Before undertaking homeschooling, parents should familiarize themselves with the laws of their state by contacting their state department of education. Updated reports on the status of these laws may be obtained from The National Legal Association, P.O. Box 2241, Santa Fe, New Mexico 87504, or The Rutherford Institute, P.O. Box 510, Manassas, Virginia 22110.

HOMESCHOOLING PERMITTED:

Alaska, Arizona, Colorado, Connecticut, Delaware, District of Columbia, Georgia, Hawaii, Idaho, Indiana, Louisiana, Maine, Massachusetts, Mississippi, Missouri, Montana, Nevada, New Jersey, New Mexico, New York, Ohio, Oklahoma, Oregon, Pennsylvania, Rhode Island, South Carolina, South Dakota, Utah, Vermont, Washington, West Virginia, and Wisconsin.

HOME MUST BE REGISTERED OR INCORPORATED AS A PRIVATE SCHOOL:

Arkansas, California, Illinois, Kansas, Kentucky, Maryland, Minnesota, Nebraska, North Carolina, Tennessee, Texas, and Virginia.

CERTIFIED TEACHER REQUIRED:

Alabama, Florida, Iowa, Michigan, and North Dakota.*

HOMESCHOOLING NOT PERMITTED:

New Hampshire and Wyoming.

---

*North Dakota also requires that the home be registered as a private school.

APPENDIX 6

Selected Resources

Homeschooling Newsletters

There are at least two dozen local and national newsletters currently being published. They range from two-page mimeographed sheets to a few larger commercial endeavors, and vary widely in ideology, educational philosophy, and quality. Some of the most consistently useful are:

California Coalition Communications Network. John Boston's organization is more generally tied into the alternative education movement. A thoughtful, unpretentious publication. P.O. Box 92, Escondido, CA 92025.

The Chalkboard. "A publication of the home-taught kids special interest group" of American Mensa, Ltd. Holly Sullivan, Coordinator, Box 1043, Vashon Island, WA 98070.

Growing Without Schooling. For over ten years the leading homeschooling publication. Founded by the late John Holt. 729 Boylston St., Boston, MA 02116.

Home Education Magazine. Homeschooling and educational issues and how-to-do-it from a variety of perspectives. Well-done, balanced coverage. Penny Barker conducts a lively "In Our Experience" forum in each issue. P.O. Box 1083, Sonasket, WA 98855.

Manas. A weekly not limited to homeschooling or education, but a regular column, "Children and Ourselves," is one of the best sources of information on educational issues of interest to homeschoolers. Highly recommended. Box 32112, El Sereno Station, Los Angeles, CA 90032.

Parent Educator and Family Report. The best-known of the religious homeschooling newsletters. Published by Raymond and Dorothy Moore. Box 9, Washougal, WA 98761.

Supplies and Materials

Although there are dozens of purveyors of "teaching tools," "educational software," "instructional materials," and school supplies of all kinds, homeschoolers will find that most of their products are oriented to the classroom mass market and are of little value in an individualized learning program. The following regularly issued catalogs of carefully evaluated children's books *are* worth obtaining, however:

Children's Books. A Clean Well-Lighted Place, 601 Van Ness, San Francisco, CA 94102. Free.

A Child's Collection. 611 Broadway, Room 708, New York, NY 10012. $2.00.

A Child's Garden. 920 St. Helena Avenue, Santa Rosa, CA 95404. Free.

Kids Line Nursery Books. 4430 School Way, Castro Valley, CA 94546. Free.

The Science Man, 4738 N. Harlem Avenue, Harwood Heights, IL 60656, offers a wide range of especially good science books.

Jerryco, 601 Linden Place, Evanston, IL 60202, regularly offers unusual science paraphernalia in an off-beat catalogue (50¢).

APPENDIX 7

Daffodils and Diesels

I'm not very good in school. This is my second year in the seventh grade, and I'm bigger than most of the other kids. They like me all right, even though I don't say much in class, and that sort of makes up for what goes on in school.

I don't know why the teachers don't like me. They never have. It seems like they don't think you know anything unless you can name the book it came out of. I read a lot at home—things like *Popular Mechanics* and *Sports Illustrated* and the Sears catalog—but I don't just sit down and read them through like they make us do in school. I use them when I want to find something out, like a batting average or when Mom buys something second-hand and wants to know if she's getting a good price.

In school, though, we've got to learn whatever

is in the book and I just can't memorize the stuff. Last year I stayed after school every night for two weeks trying to learn the names of the presidents. Some of them were easy, like Washington and Jefferson and Lincoln, but there must have been thirty altogether and I never did get them straight. I'm not too sorry, though, because the kids who learned the presidents had to turn right around and learn all the vice-presidents. I am taking the seventh grade over, but our teacher this year isn't interested in the names of the presidents. She has us trying to learn the names of all the great American inventors.

I guess I just can't remember names in history. Anyway, I've been trying to learn about trucks because my uncle owns three and he says I can drive one when I'm sixteen. I know the horsepower and gear ratios of twenty-six American trucks, and want to operate a diesel. Those diesels are really something. I started to tell my teacher about them in science class last week when the pump we were using to make a vacuum in a bell jar got hot, but she said she didn't see what a diesel engine had to do with our experiment on air pressure, so I just shut up. The kids seemed interested, though. I took four of them around to my uncle's garage after school and we watched his mechanic tear down a big diesel engine. He really knows his stuff.

I'm not very good in geography, either. They call it economic geography this year. We've been studying the imports and exports of Turkey all week, but I couldn't tell you what they are. Maybe the reason is that I missed school for a couple of days when my uncle took me downstate to pick up some livestock. He told me where we were headed and I had to figure out the best way to get there and back. He just drove and turned where I told him. It was over 500 miles round-trip and I'm figuring now what his oil cost and the wear and tear on the truck—he calls it depreciation—so we'll know how much we made.

When we got back I wrote up all the bills and sent letters to the farmers about what their pigs and cattle brought at the stockyard. My aunt said I made only three mistakes in 17 letters, all commas. I wish I could write school themes that way. The last one I had to write was on "What a daffodil thinks of Spring," and I just couldn't get going.

I don't do very well in arithmetic, either. Seems I just can't keep my mind on the problems. We had one the other day like this:

> If a 57-foot telephone pole falls across a cement highway so that $17\frac{3}{4}$ feet extend from one side and $14\frac{16}{17}$ feet extend from the other, how wide is the highway?

That seemed to me like an awfully silly way to get the width of a highway. I didn't even try to answer it because it didn't say whether the pole had fallen straight across or not.

Even in shop class I don't get very good grades. All of us kids made a broom holder and a bookend this semester and mine were sloppy. I just couldn't get interested. Mom doesn't use a broom any more with her new vacuum cleaner, and all of our books are in a bookcase with glass doors in the family room. Anyway, I wanted to make an end gate for my uncle's trailer, but the shop teacher said that meant using metal and wood both, and I'd have to learn how to work with wood first. I didn't see why, but I kept quiet and made a tie rack even though my dad doesn't wear ties. I made the tail gate after school in my uncle's garage, and he said I saved him twenty dollars.

Government class is hard for me, too. I've been staying after school trying to learn the Articles of Confederation for almost a week, because the teacher said we couldn't be good citizens unless we did. I really tried because I want to be a good citizen. I did hate to stay after school, though, because a bunch of us guys from the Southend have been cleaning up the old lot across from Taylor's Machine Shop to make a playground out of it for the little kids from the Methodist home. I made the jungle gym out of old pipe, and the guys put me in charge of things. We raised enough money collecting scrap this month to build a wire fence clear around the lot.

Dad says I can quit school when I'm sixteen. I'm sort of anxious to because there are a lot of things I want to learn to do, and, as my uncle says, I'm not getting any younger.

—Author unknown